THE ESSENTIAL PARENT'S GUIDE
to kick-starting your college student's career and
helping them land a job by graduation day.

THE UNEMPLOYED GRAD!

..and, what PARENTS can do about it!

This book is for all parents!

- Parents who have students just **entering college.**

- Parents who have students <u>in college</u>.

- Parents who have students graduating.

- Parents who have a graduate **living at home on the couch!**

DON PHILABAUM

2012 EDITION

Unless your student takes ownership of his or her career early in the college experience he or she will have a:

- 80-85 percent chance of moving home after graduation

- 70-80 percent chance of being unemployed on graduation day

- Probability of taking 7.4 months to get a job

- A 60 percent chance of having to take a job - unrelated to his or her degree!

This book will provide you a reality check on what your graduate will face upon graduation and provide tips, ideas, and best practices you can use to be a resource in their first professional job search.

THE UNEMPLOYED GRAD!

The vast majority of colleges do not require students to explore career opportunities, or develop career plans implement job search strategies. As a result, grads invest little time picking up the knowledge and skills they need to get jobs.

That's bad news for them, because the Department of Labor suggests they will go through the job search process up to 14 times by the time they are 38 years old!

This book will share with you why you need to take <u>an active role in helping your student explore career opportunities, develop a career plan and implement a job search strategy</u>.

You'll learn how to be a coach, and what to expect of your student, plus, you'll learn dozens of new, innovative yet proven job search strategies your graduate will need to know, including information about:

Social Media

Facebook

LinkedIn

Twitter

Online Communities

Job Boards

Keywords in resumes

You'll learn a lot to use in your future job searches too!

Book Production

First Edition Printing	- May 2012
Cover Design by Daniel Yeager	- daniel@nu-imagedesign.com
Interior Illustrations by Leo Michael	- leo@leomichael.com
Book Editing by Ashley Justice	- ashley@justicewebsites.com
Book Layout and Design by Daniel Yeager	- daniel@nu-imagedesign.com

Ordering Information:

> Quantity sales and special discounts are available on quantity purchases by corporations, associations, and others. For details, contact the publisher at the address above.

> Orders by U.S. trade bookstores and wholesalers.

Printed in the United States of America by CreateSpace

FOREWORD

Ben Casnocha

Co-Author

The Start-Up of You: *Adapt to the Future, Invest in Yourself,
and Transform Your Career*

Greetings parents!

In *The Start-Up of You*, Reid Hoffman (co-founder / chairman of
LinkedIn) and I assert that *everyone* is born with entrepreneurial
instincts, and that today's competitive landscape requires each of us to
re-discover these instincts and develop modern entrepreneurial skills in
order to succeed in our careers.

Don understands these changes and challenges. As he suggests,
graduates can no longer "wing it" during interviews or expect jobs
simply because they have a college degree. According to his research,

fully 95% of graduating college students do not have written career or job search plans. Students graduating today <u>need to understand their competitive assets and develop strategies around how to deploy them</u>.

If your son or daughter will lead the life you hope for him or her, he or she also needs to take ownership of a career and be prepared to drive it forward on an on-going basis in the future. Don reports that according to the US Department of Labor, your student will have held 10-14 jobs by the time he or she is just 38 years old.

As a parent, you want your kids to have a successful career. But that won't happen unless you help them. Don says in this book that many students graduate without having the mindset or skill sets necessary for career success. It's true.

In *The Start-Up of You*, we emphasize the concept of Permanent Beta: you are never a finished product. You should always be investing in yourself. Don's book is a great way to invest in your child's future. It is jammed with tips about how to use social media, how to be a positive coach, and how to navigate the application process. The best practices and strategies here will help your child find the career he or she deserves.

All the best to you and your family in journey ahead,

Ben

TESTIMONIALS

"Parents wanting to help their unemployed graduate sons or daughters cannot do better than taking the advice found in this book. The 50 Strategies to Standout are the best way to move a career forward from the beginning." **Gerry Crispin, co-founder of CareerXroads**

"Students (and parents) invest in college in search of a successful career. Unfortunately, as is pointed out in *The Unemployed Grad!,* students often leave college without a clear understanding of what career paths are best for them or how to even search for jobs. This book provides a clear path that parents and students can use to help guide their paths in developing a career plan." **Dr. Tony Alessandra, author of *The Platinum Rule* and *Communicating at Work***

"As a veteran of the college and career counseling space, Don Philabaum has his thumb on the pulse of the many challenges new grads face today as they enter what can be a confusing, intimidating job market. This book will help parents have thoughtful discussions with their soon-to-fly-the-coop grads without seeming overbearing or out of touch. And the best part? It may even help with your next career move, too." **Jenny Blake, author *Life After College***

"As a LinkedIn profile writer and an independent LinkedIn consultant, I am often asked to speak at colleges and universities about using Social Media for career development. In this harsh economy, students need every advantage to stand out in the job search.   If you have a student entering college, in college, or out of college, this book is required reading. Philabaum outlines what parents and their students need to know to build successful career plans and job search strategies." **Donna Serdula, LinkedIn-Makeover.com, author, speaker, Social Media Advisor**

"*The Unemployed Grad* touches on all of the elements parents of students transitioning from college to career need to understand to help their children succeed in this economy. It does a great job of informing parents about the key aspects -- and obstacles -- their students will face as they attempt to make the move from student to employee. As Don notes, 'This isn't your father's job search.' Job seekers today need to understand how to use social media and be able to create a strong digital footprint. I recommend parents of college students make a point to read this book; you may be surprised at what you learn, but you won't be sorry." **Miriam Salpeter, author, *Social Networking for Career Success* and *100 Conversations for Career Success.***

"Parents assume their student will not only get a degree when they leave college, but also a job that will launch their career. Unfortunately, The Unemployed Grad shares research that shows graduates are, "clueless on how to find a job". Parents will love the free workbook, career preparedness quiz and 50 plus strategies that will make their student stand out in their job search."

- **Katherine Miracle**, author of *Discovering Your Dawn, Only when you find your dawn can you unlock your true potential*

INTRODUCTION

Don Philabaum

I've been working in various businesses in the higher education industry since I graduated from college in 1975.

The first business I founded photographed graduates as they received their diplomas on graduation day at 500 colleges and high schools around the country. That led to my second business where we created alumni online communities for over 300 alumni associations worldwide, which finally led me to start a company that provides virtual career curriculum to 1,000 career centers around the world.

In each of these businesses, I found myself observing and pondering ways in which colleges and universities could do more to help graduates and alumni in the transitions in their lives.

I wrote whitepapers, reports and a book (*Alumni Online Engagement*) about how the alumni association could engage and network alumni online.

The more I got involved with career centers, the more I realized how under staffed and underfunded they were.

In reaction, I wrote a 30 page report, "*10 Ways to Get More Resources for Your Career Center.*" As I got into longer discussions with career center directors, I began to understand that even if they had more resources, they would still not be able to get students to use them.

You see, career centers are like campus clubs. They are voluntary and --as a result-- students barely use them. I'll share stats with you later that will scare you into action!

All of this activity led me to realize that colleges and universities are not focused on the career center, and maybe they never will be!

So, I wrote a 70 page report, "*Create a Career Centered College Culture and Curriculum*" that was targeted to upper management to offer 12 ways to change the culture on campus to one that focused more on careers and REQUIRED students to take OWNERSHIP of career exploration, job search strategy and career management.

Well, you probably know what is coming next…

After introducing the report and engaging in discussions with campus administrators, I started to realize that by the time colleges implemented ANY of the strategies, graduates today and subsequent classes will continue to enter the workforce ***clueless about how to look for a job.***

So I wrote a book.

This book! …and I wrote it for you, so you can step in and be a resource, partner and coach to your student as he or she builds a successful career strategy.

To my wife, Gae, and children, April, Ben and Annie, who continue to give me a sense of pride and encouragement that the world we live in will continue to become a healthier, kinder and more productive experience for everyone.

CONTENTS

TIPS ON READING THIS BOOK

Feel free to drop in and out of any chapter. Start where you want, skip and go on to whatever interests you.

This is not a sprint - it's a marathon, a continual process!

I guarantee this book will open your eyes and help you realize that you have to be a part of your student's career development and management process.

Chapter 1 & 2

In Chapter 1 you'll find out why I passionately believe you need to step in and make sure your student has the skills to search for a job. Chapter 2 goes into probably too much detail about why colleges are not focused on giving your grad the knowledge and skills he or she needs to get a job, but I thought if I did, <u>you might start your own conversation with your student's administration and encourage those folks to focus more on career exploration, job search strategies and career management</u>.

If I get too boring for you, just skip it.

Chapter 3 - 11

In the third chapter I'll encourage you to step in to not only require your student to actively explore career options, develop a job search strategy and manage his or her career, but to coach him or her along the way. You'll learn in the fourth and subsequent chapters <u>how dramatically the employment/job search industry has changed,</u> and why the current economic climate will negatively affect your grad's career for the next decade.

The book is full of important information you can use to have "thoughtful discussions" with your student. **You will find many of the strategies helpful in your own job search as well.**

Workbook

You can download a free copy of *The Unemployed Grad Workbook* by going to:

www.theunemployedgrad.com

I strongly urge you to take the time to hold discussions with your student, do some research and learn more about what we cover in each chapter. The workbook will come in handy to help you document your thoughts. By investing a small amount of time, you will be in a better position to help your student develop a written career strategy that can include:

- Inventorying current skills, behaviors, and personality traits; and identifying the careers in which they have the best opportunities to succeed.

- Learning the knowledge and techniques necessary to search for and get a job.

- Using social media, Facebook, LinkedIn, Twitter & online communities.

- Building and managing a professional network using alumni.

- Creating a personal brand that will help your graduate stand out.

- Over 60 proven strategies and techniques.

All set?

Let's get going!

YOUR GRAD WILL BE CLUELESS ABOUT HOW TO FIND A JOB

Grads will invest little time and effort exploring careers and developing a job search strategies because it is not required to graduate.

In 1956 Rudolf Franz Flesch wrote a book called, *Why Johnny Can't Read, and What You Can Do About It.* Flesch's premise was that the accepted method of teaching students how to read, the "whole word" method, did not fit everyone's learning style.

The "whole word" method of teaching reading was introduced by Horace Mann in 1830 and popularized by the McGuffey Readers. This method required readers to memorize words by sight. The problem was, when a reader was presented with a word they did not know, they couldn't sound it out. Phonics gave the reader tools to at least be able to sound the word out.

Flesch advocated the use of phonics rather than sight reading as an alternative reading method for students that were having trouble learning to read. While the public school system was not ready to adopt or add phonetics as an alternative method for some students, parents who were concerned about their children's difficulty in reading were.

Phonics gave parents an alternative method to help their children read and a whole new cottage industry was born.

Ever heard of *Hooked on Phonics*?

Chances are you used their products to help your student get a jump start on his or her reading prior to going to school.

So what does this have to do with a job for your student?

A lot!

Phonics was not an approved teaching method at the time. It was used by parents who either wanted to give their children a jump start, or by others that saw their children failing and were desperate to do something --anything-- to help them learn to read. It required parents to step in, get involved and be a part of their learning processes.

You may not realize it yet, but your student's career with a diploma is uncertain. Since 2008, nearly 80 percent of each graduating class has been unemployed on graduation day. Recent research is showing the average graduate will take 7.4 months to get a job.

Why?

The economy is partly to blame, but I believe the real reason is that graduates have not taken ownership of their careers, have not invested in career planning while in college, and as a result are clueless about how to find a job. They are among the brightest students who ever graduated from college, but their job search skills are no more advanced than those students that graduated in the founding days of the college.

Why?

The number one reason is because the vast majority of colleges do not require students to invest in career exploration and job search. Students don't have to visit the career center, they don't have to take behavior, personality, branding or interest assessments, and they certainly don't have to create a job search/career plan.

You want proof?

If your student is in college, ask him or her how many times he or she been to the career center, or how much time he or she has spent exploring career opportunities and/or if he or she has a job search strategy.

The National Association of Colleges and Employers conducts yearly studies to benchmark the industry so they can see trends and their members can implement strategies to provide better services to their customers.

One of their surveys measures the average visits to the career centers by graduating seniors:

- 27.2% never visited the career center

- 16.1% visited once

- 18.2% visited twice

- 27.0% visited 4-6 times

- 11.6% visited 8 times

Let's make sure you understand this survey. Over 61% of graduating seniors either never went to the career center or visited two or fewer times during their senior years.

If you visited the career center for one or two hours your senior year, how much do you think you might learn?

Do you think you could have:

- Taken personality, behavior, interests, skills, and branding tests and analyzed them?

- Evaluated the industries, companies and positions that were right for you?

- Chosen the right major/career?

- Built a network of alumni as a foundation to look for jobs?

- Chosen the right career?

- Attended career fairs?

- Been interviewed by companies?

I doubt it!

Additionally, would you have picked up job search skills including how to:

- Use LinkedIn to connect with alumni?

- Use Twitter to find fast breaking job opportunities?

- Use proven techniques to scour job boards?

- Use Facebook in a job search?

- Develop an online presence?

- Learn the 15 "Soft Skills" that businesses expect graduates to have?

- Learn the common mistakes grads make and how to avoid making them?

- Learn proven job search strategies?

And, finally just how much do you think you would have learned about:

- Adapting resumes with keywords that automated resume scanners will pick?

- The basics of how to look for a job?

- How to build a professional network?

- How to interview and follow up on interviews?

- How to handle the emotional ups and downs of the job search?

Without this basic knowledge and these skills, your student is destined to make numerous mistakes, waste a lot of time on the wrong techniques, and not follow up on interviews. He or she may also procrastinate because of not knowing what to do next.

While your student knows Facebook like the back of his/her hand, he/she does not know how to use Facebook in the job search, or LinkedIn, or Twitter, or any of the rapidly emerging social media tools that are essentially reinventing how people get jobs.

I can guarantee you that in the little time seniors invest in their career planning, they will not have even touched on 2 of the 20 skills, tools and strategies we just listed. Note this is only a partial listing!

IT GETS WORSE!

Your student will be entering an economy that is going to make it harder for him or her to start off with a job that is related to his or her area of studies.

Without investing time in career exploration and job search strategies, there is a good chance he or she will be represented by these stats:

- Research is showing millennials that graduated during the recession in 2009-10 suffered a 10 percent "penalty" in reduced starting salaries compared to those who graduated prior to that.

- The Bureau of Labor Statistics reports that 17 million people have college degrees but are working in positions that do not require one.

On top of all that, your graduate is not only competing with nearly 2 million fellow graduates, but also the graduates from the past four years that are struggling to start their careers, as well as the 13 million people who are currently unemployed. (some suggest that number is closer to 22 million when you add in the 7 million employed part-time due to the economy and the 2.4 million marginally attached to the workforce!)

This is giving grads fewer opportunities, lowering their expectations and, offering them less hope than the generations before them. To adjust to these new realities they are altering their goals and life plans and pushing back the five milestones of adulthood: completing school, leaving home, becoming financially independent, marrying, and having kids.

- 12 percent are finding roommates to share cost of living expenses.

- 15 percent are delaying marriage.

- 60 percent of students will take jobs completely unrelated to their major.

- 80 percent or more will be moving home for a while!

- ...and a newly released study by the Pew Research Center shows that 24% took an unpaid job just to get some experience.

How would you like to graduate into this environment?

Your student is facing enormous challenges and yet your child has invested virtually no time by graduation day to pick up the skills and knowledge he or she will need.

You probably are familiar with the phrase, "Work smarter, not harder!" That's what we want every graduate to be able to do with his or her career. By developing a career plan, your grad will ultimately spend less time and effort to find the very best job that matches his or her career goals.

But your grad is not going to be able to do that on his or her own.

You need to require your child to take ownership of his or her career and get involved in helping him or her explore career options and develop a career plan and job search strategy.

PARENTS TAKE A BACK SEAT - ASSUMING THE COLLEGE IS COVERING THIS

Despite how ugly the market is, and how much families have invested in their students' educations, most parents are taking a back seat to their students' job searches because they:

- Mistakenly think the college will prepare students for job searches.

- Feel out of touch about how to search for a job today, having limited understanding of how to use social media, personal branding and internet strategies.

- Assume their students will figure it out!

Now is NOT the time to take a back seat.

I can pretty much guarantee your grad will be clueless about how to search for a job by graduation day, but it doesn't have to be that way.

If your student is heading off to college, you have an opportunity to help him or her carefully craft a career plan while he or she is in college, and during summer breaks. If your student is in his or her senior year and/or has graduated, you still have an opportunity to step in to help your child build a job search strategy that will launch a career.

It won't take much time, but it will take a commitment on both your part and the part of your student. The really great thing is, along the way, you will also learn how you can market yourself in an industry that is changing overnight. If you expect to be back in the job market in the next 5 years, this information will be invaluable to you, too!

YOU NEED TO BE YOUR CHILD'S CAREER COACH

You know your student better than most and have more invested in his or her education than anyone else. You are the perfect person to step in and help your child build the strategies that will guide his or her career.

This book is designed to give you ideas on how you can:

- Guide

- Support

- Prod

- Encourage

- Coach

You will help your student through the process of career exploration and developing a job search strategy. You've been there for your child throughout his or her entire life; now is not the time to sit back and let your child figure this out on his or her own.

Without your help, your child will start a career lacking confidence, confused, and in many cases, disappointed that the time, effort, and investment they (AND you) made, was wasted. Matthew Segal, the founder of Our Time, a national membership organization for young people under 30 suggests students are looking for help.

> *"I can assure you that few people in my generation are living high on the hog in their parents' house,"* He says he resents the popular characterization of 20-somethings as lazy and unmoored, *"Trust me, they're not getting too comfortable sleeping in their childhood bedroom or eating out of their parents' fridge. They're moving home because they don't have jobs and they have a lot of debt."*

It's not students' fault!

Remember, the college will not require them to invest time in career planning, so they will invest their time in what the college expects of them.

In hindsight, there is evidence of their regret.

Studies show that graduates wished they had been more focused on career exploration and developing job search strategies prior to graduation day. A survey conducted by Adecco showed that 71 percent of recent college graduates wished they had done something different to prepare for the job market.

Additionally the survey found:

- 26% wished they had started their job search earlier – while in college.

- 26% wished they had spent more time networking.

- 26% wished they had applied for more jobs.

- 43% were currently working at a job that did not require a college degree.

SUMMARY

Your students will be starting their careers, knowing about as much about how to find a job as the first graduates from their college knew. By not exploring career options and developing a career and job search plans, they will join the ranks of millions of graduates who have gone before them and struggle through job searches and wander through their careers.

That is--unless you step in and help-- perhaps like you did when you provided tutoring, computer learning programs and alternative reading programs like *Hooked on Phonics*!

Think about what we've already discussed:

- 80 percent of graduates are unemployed on graduation day.

- The job search process has been revolutionized by online communities and social media.

- 71 percent of graduates wish they had worked more on their career plans while in college.

Your student has a 55% chance of graduating from college, but a degree does not come with a guarantee he or she will have a job by graduation day, or even one related the career he or she envisioned. If you want your child to start off in a career, you need to get your student to take ownership of it the minute he or she is accepted to college.

That's the easy part! Keep reading and I'll show you how!

COMING UP

I debated whether I should include the next chapter but I've gotten so much feedback from parents and students that I decided to include it. Colleges and universities do not require a graduate to invest in exploring career opportunities, create a career plan or employ a job search strategy.

I'm going to share with you why this is and hope that you will contact college administrators to encourage them to REQUIRE students to invest time in career exploration, creating career plans and job search strategies.

If you find it boring just skip it!

The truth is, I was afraid the day I walked into Stanford. And I was afraid the day I walked out.

- Carly Fiorina, CEO Political Candidate

YOUR TO DO'S AND NOTES!

_____

_____

_____

_____

_____

_____

_____

_____

_____

_____

CHAPTER RESOURCES

Visit Your College Career Center!

The Unemployed Grad Workbook

www.theunemployedgrad.com

Essential Workbook provides exercises for each chapter that will help your student build a successful career plan and job search strategy. Free!

COLLEGES & STUDENTS ARE NOT FOCUSED ON CAREER MANAGEMENT

Parents mistakenly think their students will pick up all they need to know to choose the right career and build a career plan and a job search strategy at college.

The John J. Heldrich Center for Workforce Development issued a report entitled, "Unfulfilled Expectations: Recent College Graduates Struggle in a Troubled Economy." The report that surveyed students who had graduated between 2006 and 2010 showed that:

> 58% of the graduates did not think their career centers did well in preparing them for job hunting.

I'm not convinced that colleges are completely to blame. Students and parents share some of the blame too!

Remember the survey we mentioned in the first chapter that showed 61% of graduating seniors either never went to the career center or visited two or fewer times? As we discussed in that chapter, it's nearly impossible for a student to pick up the knowledge and skills he or she will need by investing so little time in developing a job search strategy.

I think the root of the problem lies in the culture of the college, the lack of resources provided to the career center, and the fact that colleges don't require students to take ownership of their careers and lay out specific requirements they MUST complete in order to receive their degrees.

Why is that?

Well, first, we have to keep in mind that the principal mission of colleges and universities is to make sure students have completed the required curriculum to qualify for their degrees.

The mission of the college is not to get your son or daughter a job! As a result, the vast majority of colleges and universities do not require students to explore careers and build job search strategies.

It's optional. The career center is just like a club. They have to market to attract members!

Students don't have to visit the career center, don't have to build a network with alumni, don't have to learn how to professionally network, and don't have to develop a career plan.

FIVE AREAS THAT WOULD HELP THE CAREER CENTER PREPARE STUDENTS

There are five areas on which colleges could focus to give all students the kind of attention, skills, knowledge, and training they need to compete in today's uncertain job market:

- Change the culture
- Increase staff
- Career curriculum

- 24/7/365

- Analyze results

CHANGE THE CULTURE

A great place for a career center is in the Student Union where students are frequently.

However, many careers centers are located on the edges of campuses, in converted boiler rooms, in the oldest buildings on campus, or rooms about 3 times the size of a hotel room (1,200 square feet).

Career centers are not at the center of a college experience and we'd like to see that change. To do so, the colleges would need to integrate career planning into their campus cultures and curriculums.

At nearly all colleges I've been to, I've been told that the faculty controls the curriculum and sets the requirements of knowledge and skills students will need in order to graduate with degrees in their fields of expertise.

Over the decades and through hundreds of hours of discussion and arguments, they have collectively built a blue print, that when followed, results in grads being able to walk across the stage on graduation day. In some majors, there is little room for exploring personal interests and passions. (I was fortunate in my major to take music appreciation, geology, and an assortment of other courses that just "interested me." My son who graduated from Miami University's Farmer School of Business had a very tightly designed course schedule that did not give him much flexibility to veer out of the recommended courses that qualified him to graduate in four years.) As a result, there is little to no room in those total hours required to graduate to drop in additional required courses in career management.

Because of this, colleges can't demand students complete a 12-hour curriculum that focuses on career exploration and building a career plan. If students were required to complete a curriculum focused on career development and management it would have to be on their own time.

And there is evidence of that already being done on campus.

MANY COLLEGES REQUIRE COMMUNITY SERVICE HOURS

In the mid to late 90's, high schools and colleges had a huge upswing in administrations mandating students to complete a specific number of "community service" hours in order to graduate.

In Nassau County, New York, the Roslyn and Hewlett-Woodmere districts approved a program that required students beginning with the class of 1997 to take a one-semester, half-credit, community-service course and to complete a minimum of 30 hours of field work to graduate. (This was raised to 40 hours for the next class.) A neighboring county, Suffolk, instituted a similar program. Then Superintendent John G. Barnes was quoted to say, "We believe that community service is a must for all students."

The experiments in developing mandated community service programs at the local level bubbled up to the state level.

In 1997, the state of Maryland instituted a statewide mandatory community service high school graduation requirement. The law stipulated that students who attend public high schools complete a minimum of 75 community service hours.

A student reflected on first hearing about this requirement at a school assembly:

> "I heard our principal say - Look to your left, look to your right. I guarantee some of you won't graduate because of the community service requirement. You can be a 4.0 student and get into any college you want, but you won't graduate because of the community service requirement."

Even without mandated community service programs, as the admissions process to college became more competitive, students were advised to complete community service in order to improve their chances of being admitted. It became yet another opportunity for a student to show a college why they should be accepted.

As a result of political, cultural and legislative focus on community service, the number of college students who participated in community service has steadily increased over the past two decades. According to the Cooperative Intuitional Research Program, about one-third of first-year college students graduated from high schools with some type of requirement for service.

Most colleges embraced community service as a founding principal of their institutions. Harvard and Yale were founded to educate missionaries who could spread out into the distant areas of the growing United States and carry the Presbyterian message. The College of William and Mary was founded to produce graduates that could minister to Indians and attempt to convert them to Christianity.

Look at the missions of almost any college and you will see community service being an important part of the college culture. Some, like the high schools, have mandated that students complete a minimum number of community service hours in order to graduate.

- Tougaloo College, requires students to complete 60 hours of community service that is approved by the chair of their department by graduation.

- Mercy College of Health Sciences requires students to complete a 20-hour community service project. The project includes volunteering and submitting a report about the activity. There is no grade or there are no credit hours provided.

- Southern University in Louisiana, a public university, requires 60 hours of community service in order to graduate. The college has actually created community service classes that teach community engagement.

- Liberty University has required community service of their students since it was founded and offers over 350 different locations for students to volunteer. They also require students to complete two 1-hour community services classes the first year of full time enrollment.

- The University of Redlands requires students to take a 3-unit service activity course that places students in programs focused on homeless shelters, pre-schools, police departments, safe-havens and various other non-profit agencies. Each year students invest over 60,000 hours in these programs

- Loyola College offer students the Loyola4Chicago program as one of many channels to volunteer. Students agree to spend 4 hours per week in service teams at various sites, including work with children, immigrants, persons with mental illness, persons experiencing homelessness, and others in need.

- Eastern Connecticut State University offers students regular events that build camaraderie and positive community experiences through their Poverty Marathon and Day of Giving events.

- George Washington University organizes an annual Freshman Day of Service. The event focus changes from year to year but immediately indoctrinates students into a culture on of giving back to the community. It's not unusual for GWU students to spend over 160,000 hours a year volunteering.

- Stanford University dedicates 22.3 percent of its work study funds toward programs that help the community and society in general. The program's dollars support autism awareness, bringing dance to prisoners, and event to greening up South African schools.

- San Francisco State University, like many universities, has a department dedicated to raising awareness of community service. Their Institute for Civic and Community Engagement has over 7,000 students enrolled in their Community Service Learning program, which blends service projects with course work in order to educate and stimulate a culture of "giving back" to the communityWillamette University's Office of Community Service Learning provides a database of 250 charities and causes in which students may participate. Students have enthusiastically responded by investing 150,000 hours of community service work.

- Lee University takes a different tack and offers course credit to students who participate in or create volunteer opportunities.

- To increase awareness and participation in community service, Ohio Wesleyan University makes heroes of students who rack up the most volunteer hours. Each year, they host the "Golden

Bishops" ceremony that awards students who have been the most philanthropically engaged.

- North Carolina State University had over 21,000 students spend 330,000 hours during 2010 and 2011 helping serve disadvantaged youth and support early childhood literacy.

- Seattle University's administration made available $50,000 for college faculty and staff to implement projects and engage volunteers to support community projects.

While some might speculate that requiring students to participate in community service programs would in fact generate negative feelings toward the concept of giving back to the community, surveys indicate otherwise. Liberty University conducted a survey of students to determine if they should continue to require students to fulfill a community service requirement in order to graduate.

- Seventy percent supported the requirement to commit to volunteer hours in community service projects.

- Seventy six percent said they had a positive attitude about performing the required community service tasks.

There were a variety of reasons students offered as to why they participated which ranged from helping people to feeling good about themselves and improving the community. A small minority cited improving their resumes.

To help colleges and universities advance their strategies and operate as clearing houses of best practices and resources, a national organization called Campus Compact was founded in 1985 by Brown, Georgetown and Stanford Universities.

There are currently 1,200 colleges and universities that belong that represent 6 millions students. The program reaches to the highest level of the university-- the presidents-- to help drive the message throughout their cultures and continue to support the initiatives and events that drive student engagement in volunteer programs.

In fact Campus Compact developed a statement of purpose which it asks the presidents of its member intuitions to agree to. The President's Declaration on Civic Responsibility of Higher Education offers a foundation for the organization and a presidents' commitment to community engagement. In the Presidents' Statement of Principles, the first principles highlight their commitments:

> Campus Compact presidents strongly advocate the participation of students, faculty, staff, and higher education institutions in public and community service. Such service may range from individual acts of student volunteerism to institution-wide efforts to improve the social and economic well-being of America's communities.

And it works!

The total value of service contributed by students at Campus Compact member schools is estimated to be over 7 billion dollars based on the 377 million volunteer service hours contributed each year.

SO WHY DID I COVER SO MUCH DETAIL HERE?

I hope I didn't lose you in all the detail and information shared on colleges' and universities' commitments to community service. These practices and college commitment are admirable and necessary. The students who donate the hours and are the backbones of the programs are to be commended for their participation, regardless of whether it is required or not.

My goal in giving you all of this detail is to show how embedded in the college culture the concept of community service is. In the examples I shared above:

1. Colleges that set specific hours required for students to graduate.

2. That funding is provided to support new initiatives and staffing for volunteer projects.

3. Administrators at the highest levels are actively participating in promulgating the culture

While volunteerism is important, in my opinion the career center and career development should be at the center of the college experience. Everything a student does-- every club, organization, work-study program, course and activity-- should tie in to the relevance of the end game, giving grads the practical skills to search for and get jobs.

I'd like to see the presidents of all colleges and universities sign a President's Declaration of Commitment to Career Planning and Management, like they did for community service when they joined Campus Compact. That declaration would signal the importance those presidents place on increasing the number of grads who get jobs within their career fields of choice and getting those jobs by or soon after graduation day.

You can help this happen. Contact your college administrators and ask them to participate.

COLLEGES AND UNIVERSITIES WILL HAVE TO CHANGE THEIR CULTURES

A growing number of business leaders, parents and students are taking the position that the colleges' principal roles for these students is to help them get jobs, great paying jobs so they can lead successful careers and afford to be a part of the American dream, not to mention be able to afford to pay off student loans!

In fact, a UCLA survey issued in February 2012 showed that the nation's current college freshmen increasingly view bachelors' degrees as necessary tickets to better jobs. The survey found:

- 85.5% of first-year students across the country felt that being able to land a good job is a very important reason for attending college (up from 70.4% in 2006).

- 79.6% of the students indicated that becoming very well off financially is an "essential or very important" objective for them.

It's evident that students are looking for a return on their very expensive investments. There is a good chance focusing more on career planning will benefit colleges too.

- As they improve their graduation employment rates, the admissions offices will be able to use these numbers to increase enrollment.

- Working and more successful alumni are able to give back to the college.

- Students that are focused on their careers will be more likely to graduate.

Changing the focus to careers on campus will take time. If you are reading this today, your graduate will not benefit from the results, which is why we are suggesting you and your student take ownership of his or her career immediately!

INCREASE STAFFING

Colleges tend to invest more in the revenue side of their businesses then they do in the career centers, which are regarded as a cost centers.

For example, thirty percent of admissions offices have 20 or more staff members, with the average having 10-15 employees focused on recruitment. One bad admissions cycle could hurt a college, so the President's office tends to give this staff whatever it needs to fill the admissions pipeline.

Compare that to information provided to U.S. News & World Report that shows the average private college has 1 faculty to 14.8 students.

Now let's look at the career center. According to the National Association of College and Employers (NACE), the average career center has 1,645 students to one full-time staff person. On average, schools with fewer than 1,000 students have 366 students to one full-time staff person, while the ratio at schools with more than 20,000 students is 5,876 students to one full time staff person.

So it's pretty clear, the larger the college, the less likely students are to have access to, or utilize staff to help them develop their career strategies. Not having enough staff limits the amount of time career center counselors can dedicate to one-on-one counseling with any student.

How much time do they have? Let's take a look!

First we have to subtract vacations, holidays and ramp up time for each semester and eliminate the summer months. Then we have to subtract meetings, personal days, conferences, and time to prepare reports. Let's assume these things only take 30 percent of the available time.

So, assuming a career counselor is working a 40 hour week, 70 percent of his or her time would be available for available for career coaching and advising--that's only 28 hours (or 112 hours a month).

Now that we have a baseline of 112 hours x 6 months, we get 674 hours available within a school year. If we assume the college graduates 400 students, that leaves a mere 1.6 hours available to those staff members to learn about these students and what they want to achieve, and then provide meaningful guidance. Career professionals would love to spend more time coaching students, but it won't happen unless you encourage college management to give them the resources and commitment to require students to invest time in their career planning.

It's clear that career centers will need more staff to invest more time in students should they decide to require students to explore career options and build job search strategies. The likelihood of that happening soon though is slim, as the average career center has been forced to take 4.2 percent in budget cuts over the last two years.

CAREER CURRICULUM

A typical state college has at least 20,000 students. One that we looked at had over 1,800 courses and 200 majors. The selection of courses taught by the 1,000-member faculty is literally breathtaking. So is the campus!

At a time when all colleges and universities are ramping up their online course selection as a way to handle an overflow and influx of students, as well as reach out to a global audience of students, virtually none have developed courses that focus on the primary skills students need in searching for jobs.

Our surveys of colleges found a limited number that have invested in developing professional career curriculum in:

- Choosing a career

- Resume development

- Job search skills

- Career management

- Networking

- Use of social media including Twitter, YouTube and personal websites

- Use of LinkedIn & Facebook

- Building a personal brand

- Interviewing and follow up skills

- Soft skills like communication, leadership, ethics, dress and showing up on time

The career center provides the traditional services that include access to assessments as well as career fairs, meetings with hiring managers, resume development, mock interviewing, general career coaching and access to internships and job shadowing opportunities. Believe me, the career center is busy!

Some colleges do give their career centers staff access to class time with faculty, but generally this is for a quick one-off presentation, meaning they can't cover as much or as in depth as they might like to.

To help career centers achieve their mission, college administrators will need to require career courses be taken by students starting their freshmen years.

But recent studies by N.A.C.E suggest this is not going to happen anytime soon. Their recent yearly benchmark survey suggests:

- A decline in services, driven largely by the bigger colleges. For example, the average number of workshops delivered fell from 73-61

- In 2010-2011, an average of 344 students were assisted with employer-based internships, down from an average of 426 in 2009-10

With all colleges facing budget pressures, and career centers facing yearly budget cuts, it's unlikely they will have the resources to invest in career curriculum.

24/7/365

Students' behaviors are changing rapidly and they are learning that taking online courses at any time, from any place, and on any device is a plus for them. They also like the fact that they can replay a video presentation, read the transcript of an online presentation and through their social networks, and/or ask questions they might have been too shy in class to raise a hand and ask.

My firm believes that to reach all graduates, career centers have to build scalable strategies that take advantage of students' changing behaviors, and their use of mobile devices and social media.

Another reason students are not utilizing the career centers is that the schedule of the centers is inconvenient. In some instances, the times the career center is open just doesn't work for students. Like most departments on campus, career centers are generally open at 8 am and usually close by 5:00 p.m. I heard President Obama, in a speech to University of Michigan students who got up early enough to go through security to hear the President speak at 9:00 a.m., congratulate them for being there, "having been a college student I realize 9:00 a.m. is still pretty early for most of you," he said.

Think about it. Students have classes, clubs, research, part time work, assignments and other responsibilities throughout their days, making it less likely for them to use the career center from 8:00 a.m. to 5:00 p.m., and, like most departments, very few career centers are open on weekends!

That's not the best way to serve students today.

We advocate that the career center should no longer be only a destination, or place, but it should also be "in the clouds" where all students can gain access to the services offered there 24/7, 365 days a year.

Companies like TalentMarks are designing online career tools, online chat access, and access to career courses that students can access anytime, from any device, anywhere they are – even after they graduate.

In working with colleges, we've proven that students can learn more about career exploration and job search strategies via online courses and webinars, which give the career professionals more one-on-one time to coach them. Our anytime, anywhere online career implementations show students use these services at 10:00 p.m., 11:00 p.m. and even 1:00 a.m.. We think this flexible model provides a more enriching opportunity for students to learn career strategies.

ANALYZE RESULTS

The other night, my wife and I rented Moneyball, a movie based on the book of the same name.

Moneyball is about Billy Beane, a high school baseball superstar, who, like Lebron James in basketball, bypassed college and went straight to the majors.

After a few years, management recognized they had pushed Billy too quickly into the big leagues, and he was eventually traded through a series of teams and ultimately landed in the minor leagues until he was given an opportunity to join the coaching and managing side of the business.

Billy Beane eventually became the General Manager of the Oakland A's. Oakland was a smaller market and the owner did not have unlimited resources to dump into the team.

As a result Billy could only commit 1/4th of the amount of money to salaries that other teams like the New York Yankees could. With limited money, he could not afford to sign up "big names," proven, powerful players. He had to make the best choices with a limited budget.

During a meeting with the Cleveland Indians management, he noticed a young staffer had some unorthodox opinions. Before he left their offices, he met with the young man to learn how he analyzed players. Paul DePodesta, a Harvard finance grad, had developed a formula to analyze everything about baseball--hits, errors, at bats, pitches-- and put a monetary value to the data.

Through rigorous statistical analysis, he demonstrated that on-base percentage and slugging percentage are better indicators of offensive success. After listening to this theory, Billy became convinced that these qualities were cheaper to obtain on the open market than more historically valued qualities such as speed and contact.

DePodesta's concept was revolutionary at the time. He used what is called an analytical, evidence-based, saber metric approach to assembling a competitive baseball team, despite Oakland's disadvantaged revenue situation.

Billy's implementation of this unproven strategy went against the judgment of his staff, scouts, executives, industry experts, and the media and fans. His experienced scouts, who used intuition, gut, and personal theories were aghast that he was adopting this model and ignoring their professional advice. Imagine listening to a kid fresh out of college—and a finance major at that!

Using his economic model Billy reached out to undervalued players whom he could hire for less, but had potential when put together as a team, to become successful. With only $41 million dollars available for players' salaries, he had to create a competitive team to beat the New York Yankees, a team that had $145 million dollars to spend on the top talent in the industry.

Halfway into their first season, the concept looked like a failure, but then things started to click and the team ended up competing with the New York Yankees in the World Series.

The incredible success of the Oakland A's proved a team could assemble and manage a team not based on stats, and the gut feelings of experienced recruiters, but by economic models that crunched the stats and provided information that managers could analyze to find best player combinations at the best value.

Why bring this up?

Because, in our opinion, colleges need to not only collect more data and information about student employment, but they also need to analyze the information to determine what they need to tweak, change and modify in order to get more students jobs and off to fantastic careers.

I'm having a hard time finding a college that --like Billy Beane-- is committed to analyzing graduate employment data. <u>Many gather some data, but they don't use the data to fix the fundamental problems graduates and companies are facing.</u>

There is evidence this is already happening in other departments on campus and the first one that comes to mind is the admissions office. The admissions office started analyzing things way back in the 80's and today, analytics controls everything they do.

The entire admissions and recruiting process is a numbers game and those involved in recruiting have been required over time to collect enormous amounts of data to evaluate and compare admittances, yields, summer melt and other variables. Enrollment professionals use the data to make mid-course corrections and to keep management aware of their progress.

They track and analyze everything:

- The percent of students that respond to a mailing

- Where students are in their application phases

- Who is actively looking at the college and who needs special contacts

- Which students they really want to focus on and get to the college

- Who is in the funnel

...and much more! The president receives monthly reports from his enrollment management staff keeping him/her informed of their progress and standing ready to make any budget adjustments necessary if there is a negative trend.

Admissions offices invest in analytics because they know they are in a numbers game. With the right resources, career centers could be managing and assisting students and grads so they have a better chance of getting a job by graduation day. They don't do it, because it doesn't drive revenue. However, its data you need to help decide which college to choose.

If your student has a job by the time he or she graduates, your student will (in effect) earn a full year back of his or her tuition. Keep that in mind. If you are a parent of a student in college you have the opportunity right now to intervene and help your student build a strategy that will return up to $30,000 in salary as a result.

What would you like the career center to measure? We've compiled a few things, but why not add yours?

- The number of grads with jobs on graduation day
- Percentage of students who are working within their field of study
- Average time it took grads to get a job
- Percentage of grads without a job by the 3rd, 6th, 9th and 12th months after graduation
- Percentage of grads brought into companies by fellow alumni
- Average pay of grads within majors
- Percentage of graduates defaulting on student loans

There is a good chance we will see more of this happen as congress continues to create legislation designed to make sure students can pay back their loans by acquiring "gainful employment" after graduation.

SUMMARY

Keep in mind that changes happen slowly in higher education. If your student's college does not require him or her to invest in career planning, you will need to step in and make sure your child takes ownership of his or her career!

We've looked at why colleges don't require students to explore career opportunities, or require them to build career plans. We have also discussed 5 ways colleges could focus more on preparing grads for their careers and job searches. If your son or daughter is currently in college, chances are these will not be implemented until he or she is well into a career, so it's up to you to stay focused on helping him or her build career plans.

COMING UP

You have the most time and money invested in your student. If he or she is to assume ownership of a career, your student will need your guidance and support to stay on track.

You have brains in your head.
You have feet in your shoes.
You can steer yourself in any direction you choose.
You're on your own.
And you know what you know.
You are the guy who'll decide where to go.

- Dr. Seuss

YOUR TO DO'S AND NOTES!

_____

_____

_____

_____

_____

_____

_____

_____

_____

CHAPTER RESOURCES

| *Visit Your College Career Center!* | **Career Readiness Quiz** www.theunemployedgrad.com | Most grads think they know what they need to do to search for a job. Here's a 100 question quiz that will help them see what they need to be working on today! Free! |

YOU NEED TO ASSUME THE ROLE OF "CAREER COACH"!

You've coached your student his or her entire life. Why stop now? This chapter will encourage you to require your child to assume ownership of a career and you to step in to guide and coach him or her through the process.

The other evening I was watching the TV program, *The Voice* with my wife and daughter.

Karla Davis, one of the contestants was in a coaching session with Adam Levine, (referred to as a "hottie" in our house) one of the judges of the program, and Alanis Morissette, one to the top female vocalists of the past decade. Their job was to help Karla develop her own version of Lionel Ritchie top 1977 hit, *Easy*. (It seemed like just yesterday I was listening to it!)

As they all stood around a large grand piano, Karla took a first stab at singing Lionel Ritchie's song. It came off flat and lifeless and Karla knew it.

Alanis was first to offer advice, "Whenever I try to find the right key to a song that is the Zen spot, I always go too far, and then I bring it down." Karla seemed still embarrassed from starting her session with her idol so poorly and had a confused look on her face as she tried to take in the advice Alanis was sharing.

Then Adam followed by suggesting that Karla stretch some of the notes, particularly the point where she sang E-A-S-Y! Alanis, looking for a way that Karla could step out of her normally shy personality, suggested Karla give a name to the part of her that can really belt out a chord. They decided to call that part of her being "Bertha." Adam candidly suggested that Bertha needed to be in both Karla's head and heart when she sings the big notes. Both wanted Karla to literally escape who she was to reach who she could be.

They recognized that Karla was insecure and somewhat shy and like good coaches, they were gently offering ideas and advice designed to give her more confidence so she could let her natural talent explode.

Karla tried the Lionel Ritchie song again, but this time with more confidence, more direction and more style.

You guessed it-- she nailed it and she immediately knew she just had a break through moment. Celebrating, she ran around the piano, doing high fives. Adam shared his enthusiasm raised his arms high in the air, and said, "Whatever that was, that was perfect. Just do that ALL the time!"

It took a little coaching and advice to help her reach a state of confidence she knew she could find again. Both Adam and Alanis were able to help her move beyond her fear and sense of apprehension and to push herself.

Later, after the session, Karla said, "Wow, it's like a break though for me. That's good! I think I was the biggest thing holding me back, and, now I see it more than ever! It took 20 minutes for them to make me see and hear something in me that I would never – EVER-- have been able to do on my own."

And that's what coaching can do!

Your son or daughter is a diamond in the rough.

It won't take much to help your child unlock the power and potential he or she was born with. One simple suggestion can change a life, and change THE world.

EVERYONE USES COACHES

In addition to musicians, professional athletes have them, business executives have them, and actors have them, too.

The main role of a coach is to help people maximize performances, to help them be the best they can be. Research supports that. There is evidence that career coaches can increase the number of students who stay in college by as much as 15%.

In my opinion, career coaches are the doctors of careers.

Good career coaches know how to quickly identify what will help a person break through a barrier, make a decision they have been struggling with, or discover something they were unable to admit.

Like doctors, engineers, or any other professionals, career coaches need some data, as well as some background information in order to be able to analyze a situation. Your student will get more out of sessions with coaches if he or she comes equipped with results of assessments. He or she will also gain a better understanding of himself or herself.

Unfortunately, few students avail themselves of a career coach while in college, or ever, for that matter. Many misunderstand what a career coach is. College students who have visited guidance counselors who are helping them determine which courses to take to qualify for their degrees need to know that these counselors don't have time to really get to know each student.

The same is true for career center counselors.

Career centers are so under staffed; they barely have time to help the students prepare resumes. We've not been able to find any statistics on it, but based on the number of students career centers are responsible for, and the time staff has available, we've deduced the career center staff has only 1.6 hours to spend with each student. For most, the time is spent helping students develop and improve resumes. These short task-oriented interactions color students' perceptions of what a career coach can do for them.

But a good coaching relationship is one in which a dedicated coach helps a person accomplish things he or she wants to do or helps him or her overcome issues not easily handled alone. Career coaches will help students build their strategies over time and will help them keep on track.

Coaching relationships are more about accountability and outcome. The coach helps the student identify what he/she needs to do and the steps he or she needs to accomplish that. We all need this kind of help from time to time because we are so time starved, are multi-tasking too many projects, and we easily lose sight of what the most important things to accomplish are.

There are many reasons your student may want to reach out to a coach. His or her reasons don't have to be focused on careers, but could include life coaching, relationships or personal development.

Coaches can help students:

- Explore career options

- Develop job strategies

- Organize the job search process

- Manage the campus-to-corporate transition

- Learn how to live on their own and handle finances

- Overcome the emotional highs and lows of a job search process

- Handle the debilitating effects of a personal break up or loss of a loved one

- Handle a first job

- Work in a team environment or for a boss

- Develop positive personal routines and behaviors

- Overcome compulsive behaviors.

- Handle time management better or overcome procrastination.

Career coaches easily take on these projects and help the students work through them.

FOUR YEAR COACHING PLAN

In Chapter 1, we shared with you an industry report that suggested 61 percent of graduating seniors either never went to the career center of visited once or twice. I think your student should be investing a minimum of 20-40 hours per year on career exploration, career planning and learning the tips and best practices of a job search process.

That's essentially the equivalent of a 3 credit hour course each year.

Later in Chapter 9, I'll share 15 soft skills that business executives suggest graduates lack. Soft skills include communication, leadership, work ethics, teamwork and business etiquette. I'll suggest that your student also begin his or her freshman year becoming exposed to literature, courses, articles, videos and information that will give him or her the knowledge needed to excel in these areas as well.

Both will require your student to set aside time, as if he or she were taking courses at college each week to fulfill a personal commitment to owning and managing a career strategy.

In addition to independent study and exploration, it's wise to make sure your student has access to you or a professional coach they can ask questions of.

If your student is just entering college, you have an opportunity to lay out a comprehensive career planning strategy that can involve ongoing coaching. Let's take a quick look at what coaching could do for your student.

Freshman

During the freshman year, a coach can focus on assessment analysis and career exploration. Coaches can help evaluate personality, behavior, branding and skill assessments and give your child insight on the career paths that he or she would enjoy, excel or "be a natural" at. While we don't worry too much about creating a resume during the freshman year, we want students to start thinking about what their resume will look like and what experience they will have to acquire to create a marketable resume. During the year, coaches should assign homework including research as to which careers would best fit students' personalities, behaviors, interests, and overall goals.

Sophomore

In the sophomore year, a coach can help frame what a student is learning with the realities of the work environment and continue to encourage him or her to build an online presence and professionally network. The coach should assign networking books to read and discuss who your student should be connecting with, as well as help manage those relationships. You need to encourage your student to participate in campus groups so that by the senior year, he or she will be able to take on leadership positions.

The goal is to position your student for internship opportunities during his or her sophomore and junior years. We'd also like to see students start to continue to learn and understand the soft skills we cover in Chapter 9.

Junior

As students move into their junior years, coaches should begin to prepare them for the psychological and intellectual changes they will need to make as they shift from their college experiences into work environments. More focus should be placed on building powerful resumes and using social media tools like LinkedIn, Facebook and Twitter to build an online presence and to get noticed as a credible employee. Students should be encouraged to participate in mock interviews at the career center as well as career fairs. Some employers will be looking for summer interns, so it's important to ask your student to participate.

By the end of the year, your student should have a solid foundation concerning what he or she wants to do and the types of industries and companies for which he or she wants to work.

Senior

Finally, as your student moves into his or her senior year, the coach should ensure he or she is taking the steps to have a job by graduation day.

This is the year your student should have all pistons firing on his or her job search strategy. Your student is not developing a strategy, but implementing and modifying it as needed.

Too often, students assume they'll start looking for a job after graduation. This attitude will cost $3,000 to $4,000 in lost income every month a student remains unemployed. But worse, he or she will end up doing the same thing I did-- and perhaps you did--and start looking for a job to make ends meet, not a job that will start a career.

SHOULD YOU BE THEIR COACH?

I want to make sure you have a good idea of what a coach and student relationship looks like to see if you want to "apply" for the job.

I think you can do it!

After all you've been a coach from the day your child went to kindergarten. While the college experience minimizes your ability to have day to day contact with your son or daughter, a project like this will keep you connected periodically and can be a fun activity that is easily managed.

Of course, you don't have to step in and be the career coach, you could actually hire a professional career coach to do that.

The way I see it, you have three options.

- Hire a professional career coach.

- You step in to be the career coach.

- Be the career coach, and bring in a professional when needed.

Let's take a quick look at each option.

1) Hire a professional career coach

Professional career coaches charge anywhere from $100 to $250 per hour. In my opinion, your student should have 10-15 hours of career coaching per year, and should be investing another 20-40 hours researching, networking and developing his or her career plan. You should be able to find a coach in your community that would be able to commit to managing your student's career development for the four years of college and immediately after graduation.

2) You step in as the career coach

If you have the time and the interest to step in and be the coach, I think you'll find the job fun and rewarding. More importantly, you will put yourself in a better position to maximize both your investment and your student's investment in acquiring a college degree.

This book will give you a foundation of knowledge as you assume the role of your student's career coach. In the following chapters, you'll learn how to advise your child to prepare for a drastically different job market, coach him or her to develop an online presence, and give your child tips and best practices that will help him or her get a job. You will also get to know about the dozens of things companies are looking for in a candidate and the common mistakes graduates make.

3) You be the career coach and bring in a professional for certain parts

A blended approach might be to bring in a professional career coach to help out in areas where you do not think you have enough expertise. For example, you might want to consider having a professional career coach spend time with your student to evaluate his or her assessments, and to provide feedback and to answer your student's questions. Some career coaches get certified to provide or translate specific assessments. They have a deeper understanding of the results, and as a result probably can analyze your student's assessments and provide a better review of what those assessments mean. This is a foundational step and one that I don't think you want to short change.

Or, you might want to bring in a professional career coach to help when you see your student is not picking up in a specific area. A blended strategy also gives you access to a career coach to review ideas, to "brainstorm," and talk through your student's strategy. It's always helpful to have someone with whom to discuss these issues. If you do this, make sure the coach understands what you want him or her to do and that you are interested in working with him or her for all four years of college. You want the continuity of the same career coach.

ASSUMING YOU DECIDE TO BE THE CAREER COACH!

I'm going to assume that you will take on the role of your student's career coach.

There are 6 things you need to do to formalize a coaching relationship:

1. Have a frank talk about the realities of looking for a job. Stick to the facts!

2. Your student needs to take ownership of his or her career.

3. Outline your roles and responsibilities.

4. Once you have an agreement, sign a contract.

5. Meet on a regular basis, and set time monthly and/or quarterly that you can agree on to do so.

6. Lead, don't do!

My hope is our colleges will begin to take coaching more seriously and start to inculcate an interest, desire… no, a *behavior* that includes reaching out and using coaches for personal self improvement.

1) Stick to the facts!

I like to remind students that they are entering the worst economy for graduates ever! They are competing with 13 million people out of work as well as the 2 million grads from this year and the previous 4 years.

It's brutal out there.

Students need to hear these statistics before they even go to college so they understand the RISKS of not building and managing their strategies.

- 80 percent of the last 4 graduating classes were unemployed on graduation day.

- The average grad in 2011 took 7.4 months to get a job.

- 95% of students did not have a written career plan.

- 61% of grads had only 1 mentor during college.

- 60% of students spent less than 5 hours per week on a job search.

- 60% of graduates are working in jobs unrelated to their studies.

- 58% of graduates wish they had worked more on developing a career plan while in college.

- 80% of graduates move home with their parents after college.

- You have to impress upon your child that he or she just can't "wing it" and expect to get a job.

Finally, you need to grab your child's attention and remind him or her that according to the Department of Labor, he or she will have 11-14 jobs by age of 38. Does your child really want to stumble through the next 14 job searches without really knowing what he or she is doing?

Remind your child to "Work smarter, not harder!" A little time and effort today will make his or her life immensely more productive, rewarding and fulfilling.

2) Your student needs to take ownership of his or her career

As a reminder, the reason you have to pick up this role is that your student's college does not require him or her to explore career options and build a job search strategy. It's just not part of the mission.

But it is part of yours!

If this seems right to you, and you know you can be a resource to your student, then by all means step in and help.

Your student is going to have to agree that he/she will take ownership of a career plan and follow the steps we are sharing to help him or her build it. You will get some push back from your child that he or she may not have time and that this shouldn't be his or her focus -- but you have to be firm and remind your child that he or she needs to invest the time today or risk being an unfortunate statistic tomorrow.

We know the jobs are out there:

- Each month on Craig's List there are over 2 million jobs posted.

- According to U.S. Bureau of Labor Statistics even in the worst days since our recession began in 2007, there have been an average of 3,000,000 unfilled jobs each month!

With a plan, your child has a greater chance of having a career job when he or she graduates.

3) Outline your roles and responsibilities

You also need to help your child understand your goal in helping him or her-- your goal in investing in his or her future-- is that he or she gets a job that matches your child's passions and interests and that is rewarding to him or her, regardless of the pay.

I think I can speak for you on this--you just want to see your child happy and living a fulfilling life.

Your child needs to see the wisdom of having a plan in place that makes it effortless to move through these job transitions with no interruption in pay and with the kind of career advances he or she wants.

That being said, share with your child that you want to work with him or her because the college does not prepare its students for finding a career.

Remind them that in this process:

- You are acting as a listener and a coach

- That you are NOT taking a position of telling your child what to do

- That you feel that you are stepping into the same position as a faculty member when you share interesting concepts, engage him or her in discussion, and offer advice – what your child does with this is up to him or her.

Remind your child that you do not want to take the position of a nag. This is a two-way relationship, and if your child is serious about the process, he or she will commit to what is required, just like he or she is committed to writing papers, doing research and completing assignments for classes. This will be different than course work as the results of your child's efforts will be knowledge and skills they actually use for an entire life!

A small investment today will continue to pay off for your child throughout his or her entire life.

Your job is not to choose a career, nor control the process, nor do the work. You know the issues encountered in a job search and your past experience, compassion and wisdom will help your child successfully transition to his or her first job. Plus, by the time you finish reading this book, I guarantee you'll know more about using Facebook, LinkedIn, and Social Media then your child will pick up on his or her own!

4) Sign an agreement

Both you and your student are spending a fortune and investing a great deal of time to make college happen.

While we want you to assume the role of coach for your child, we also want you to treat this like a business arrangement and have your student sign an agreement outlining expectations and responsibilities.

Your agreement should include:

- An outline of **your** responsibilities

- An outline of **your child's** responsibilities

- Details about what will be accomplished during each year of college

- Goals for each step that include *how many, when,* and *who*

- Agreed upon meeting dates to review progress

- Reports

I know it's hard to have a business relationship with your kids.

In fact it's almost impossible to keep from reacting emotionally when they are not doing what you want, but if you begin correctly, and both agree to a formal arrangement, including the responsibilities you have to one other, I'm confident you can keep things on track.

5) Meet on a regular basis

I asked you to include this in the agreement because it's a critical step in the career development process.

You need to have regular meetings to evaluate progress and measure the results against expectations.

Your role in these meetings is to listen and provide advice. There should be a set agenda which is driven by the agreement and career management strategy. Your child should provide a report to you prior to your scheduled meeting to give you time to review it and prepare your thoughts. You may do some research and find some links you want your child to check out, articles to read, videos to watch, or career curriculum courses to take.

Following the meeting, your child should send you the minutes of the meeting which include what was discussed as well as what he or she is going to accomplish prior to the next meeting.

This is nothing new. While at home, you periodically asked about their classes, what they had to do and what grades they expected to get in classes.

6) Lead - Don't Do!

The reason you picked up this book is that you want to make sure your student gets off to a great start in his or her career, but what you don't want to do is to take ownership of his or her job search.

You want to make sure your child is aware of the skills he or she will need, that your child does the research, and that he or she handles the day to day tasks that will be required to get a job.

The urge to do more can be great!

The Collegiate Employment Research Institute surveyed more than 700 employers who traditionally hire new college graduates. Their survey found that nearly one-third of the graduates' parents had submitted resumes on a child's behalf, some without even informing the child. Wow!

Another one-quarter reported hearing from parents who urged an employer to hire their son or daughter for a position. Another WOW!

And shockingly, four percent of respondents reported that a parent actually showed up for the candidate's job interview! Don't even think of that!

The report also showed parents engaged in every aspect of their graduate's employment.

- 6 percent advocated for promotion or salary increases.

- 9 percent tried to negotiate salary and benefits.

- 12 percent were involved in making interview arrangements.

- 15 percent complained if the company did not hire a student.

- 17 percent attended a career fair with a student.

- 40 percent obtained information about companies for a student.

I think it's ok to conduct some searches as long as your student is doing the same thing, but the six bulleted points above are probably not great strategies, and in the long run will hurt your student's career opportunities.

And just to be clear:

- Don't call a firm and tell them how great your kid is.

- Don't even think of going to the interview--unless you want to sit in the car!

- Don't try to negotiate pay.

Just keep in mind this is your child's job search and he or she needs to have complete ownership of it.

SUMMARY

After reading this book, I am confident you will have a greater understanding of how drastically the job search process has changed and that you will have a better idea of the risk and opportunities that your student will have. Armed with this knowledge, you will be one step ahead of your child, until he or she takes ownership and zooms past you!

We encourage you to:

- Share facts, stats and best practices.

- Open your student's eyes to opportunities.

- Listen to what he or she wants to do.

- Encourage your child to set goals and document his or her steps and grab the "brass ring" and take hold of his or her own destiny.

Just like Karla Davis discovered in the beginning of this chapter, all it takes is a few minutes with a coach to bring out a spark that not only changes your child's life, but can change the world.

Do that for your son or daughter and you will make the world and many businesses more successful and better places to work!

COMING UP

This is not your father's job search market. In just the last 4 years, the techniques and successful methods to find a job have changed. It's revolutionary! The meat of what you need to know is coming. Get your highlighter ready because we'll introduce you to dozens of new, proven strategies.

Find something you love to do and you'll never have to work a day in your life

- Harvey McKay, Author

YOUR TO DO'S AND NOTES!

_____

_____

_____

_____

_____

_____

_____

_____

_____

_____

CHAPTER RESOURCES

| *Visit Your College Career Center!* | **Career Coach Webinars**
 www.theunemployedgrad.com | You can gain the insights and advice of some of the top student/grad career coaches in the nation in these regularly scheduled webinars. |

YOUR GRADUATE IS ENTERING A HIGHLY COMPETITIVE GLOBAL LABOR MARKET - WITH NO JOB SEARCH STRATEGY!

Your graduate is going to compete with 13 million people out of work, 2 million fellow graduates, 6 million graduates from Chinese colleges and graduates and non-graduate workers from around the world!

Each year nearly 2 million new graduates hit the streets looking for a job.

I've always wondered how our economy absorbs so many new workers, not only those graduating from college, but the others who are graduating from high school and are not going to college.

Think about it, between the high school and college grads, we estimate nearly 3,000,000 people are looking for a job each June. For the better part of the past four years, our economy has shed more jobs than have been created, and even on the best month, we've barely generated more than 200,000 new jobs. It's interesting to note that EVERY decade, 1970's, 1980's and 1990's our economy produced on average about 138,000 jobs every month. However, because of the HUGE recession in 2000, that decade actually lost jobs.

A lot has changed in the employment world since 2007.

> In 2007, nearly 60% of the students graduating had jobs by graduation day. Another 15-19 percent went on to advanced degrees, which left a little over 20% without jobs. In hindsight, those were the good old days!

Today, on a nationwide basis, things have flipped.

> Only 20% of the students graduating from college have a job and 80% are unemployed or heading to graduate and professional school. It's a miserable time for graduates to be stepping into the cold, cruel world, particularly when you combine the fact that they are leaving college with the highest credit card and student loan debt of any students in the history of our country, or in fact the world.

IT'S A GLOBAL EMPLOYMENT ECONOMY

On top of that, the employment world has gone from local, regional, state, and national to global. The Internet has had much to do with enabling businesses of all sizes to find employees, either full time, part time, or job specific to handle tasks. This has not only enabled companies to hold down their costs, but also to ramp up and provide services to customers faster, with less effort.

Your student is not only competing with his or her fellow graduates, but with graduates around the globe, including the 6,000,000 students China graduates EACH year! I've heard some reports that China graduates more science and engineering students then the United States graduates students of all disciplines. In a world connected by the Internet and a common language, a company can easily get competent, degreed and English speaking workers at anytime.

Businesses do business in a global society today. They see the world not only as a source of talent, but as a customer base. The United States has only 325 million consumers, and the rest of the world has nearly 7 billion consumers!

In article by Charles Krugman in the New York Times, that he called "Made in the World," a quotation by Mike Splinter, the C.E.O. of Applied Materials, perfectly sums up why businesses reach out to talented employees around the world:

"Outsourcing was 10 years ago, where you'd say, 'Let's send some software generation overseas.' This is not the outsourcing we're doing today. This is just where I am going to get something done. Now you say, 'Hey, half my Ph.D.'s in my R-and-D department would rather live in Singapore, Taiwan or China because their hometown is there and they can go there and still work for my company.' This is the next evolution."

In the same article, Michael Dell the founder of Dell, Inc. supports our point that businesses are developing relationships and are planting their flags in other countries because they know in an expanding global marketplace, the more countries they have a presence in, the more products and services they will sell:

"I always remind people that 96 percent of our potential new customers today live outside of America." That's the rest of the world. "If companies like Dell want to sell to them," he added, "(they) need to design and manufacture some parts (and) products in their countries."

It's not just major corporations that are employing people around the world. My firms have employed people in the Philippines, India, Bosnia and even Pakistan because they had the right talent at the right price and could deliver what we needed when we needed it. Small business owners and entrepreneurs are using services like Elance, Odesk and others to hire people with master's degrees for less than five dollars per hour. The Internet and a common language are making this possible.

THEIR COMPETITION IS COMING FROM COMPUTERS TOO!

Since the 1980's, the personal computer has changed the tools used to run a business.

- Accounting and finance have shifted from hand-written ledgers to excel sheets and programs.

- Typewriters have been replaced by word-processing and computers.

- Telephones have diminished in importance and been largely replaced by more rapid communications like email and texting.

A host of other efficiencies have been introduced to make people and groups more productive as well. Along the way, these technologies flattened the corporate structure, eliminated pools of secretaries, assistants, and middle managers. What is coming next, though, could rip out entire floors of staff as computers that take no holidays, work 34/7/365, and require no health care, get smarter.

If you are around my age, you might remember the seminal 1968 movie directed by Stanley Kubrick, written by Arthur C. Clarke, where Hal the computer talks amicably, renders aesthetic judgments of drawings, and recognizes the emotional state of the crew. Hal was an important part of the team – you might say he was the brains of the astronauts - as he monitored systems, was assigned key assignments, and even had ongoing discussions with the crew members.

Then in 1997, IBM scientists built a computer they called *Deep Blue* to play chess with world champion chess player Garry Kasparov. The 1.2 ton computer's job was to out think and out analyze every move Kasparov made. The nearly decade long project enabled *Deep Blue* to examine and evaluate two to three thousand chess positions per second. With that kind of speed and focus, what chance does a mere mortal have whose thoughts might get interrupted by the attractive brunette in the audience, the cough of an official, the heat in the room, or the urge to go to the bathroom?

In the first real test of man over machine on May 11, 1997 IBM's computer *Deep Blue* beat the world chess champion after a six-game match that included two wins for *Deep Blue*, one for Kasparow, and three draws.   The match lasted several days and received massive media coverage.   It opened the door for the creativity of computer programmers to build computers as capable of handling complex calculations required to discover new drugs, handle complex modeling, or send objects out of our solar system!

Now only a decade later, computers are being introduced that will have the potential to handle white collar positions-- in secretarial, analytical, engineering and even in the health fields! Graduates and workers in engineering, accounting, finance, math, and even teaching will find computers equipped with their skills coming into to market in the next decade.

How can I predict that?

HAL'S COUSIN WATSON SETS A NEW BAR!

In September of 2011, after years of research, a team of IBM scientists and engineers created *Watson*, their latest, smartest, new "thinking computer" that competed with two of Jeopardy's top celebrated contestants, Ken Jennings and Brad Rutter.

This challenge was much greater than *Deep Blue* as the team needed to develop a computing system that could rival a human's ability to answer questions posed in natural language with speed, accuracy and confidence.   Jeopardy provides the ultimate challenge because the game's clues involve analyzing subtle meanings, irony, riddles, and other complexities in which humans excel and computers traditionally do not.

Watson had to understand the language of a clue, register the intent of the question, search millions of lines of human language, and return a single, precise answer in less than three seconds.

That is exactly what *Watson* did to win!

The computer's ability to understand the meaning and context of human language and rapidly process information to find precise answers to complex questions holds enormous potential to transform how computers help people accomplish tasks in both business and personal lives.

To me, this is further proof that our educational system no longer needs to focus on rote memorization, but should focus on how to use information and data and to think creatively and critically.

Computers built on the success of the IBM team will be displacing millions of workers in the coming decades and the only thing that will save careers will be abilities to think more creatively then the computers.

While politicians try to figure out how to find a way to bring manufacturing jobs back to America, business leaders are reminding them that it's too late. During the Super Bowl, I watched a car commercial that showed cars being built in a pristine, hospital-clean factory by robotic arms that even repaired themselves. While we worry about outsourcing jobs to other countries, at the same time--very quietly--manufacturing jobs are being outsourced to cousins of Hal the computer.

I don't hear anyone complaining.

In fact, I hear everyone talking to *Siri*, Apple's faithful assistant who receives no pay, works 24/7/365 and yet has the skills to talk to tens of millions of people around the world! My wife loves to challenge *Siri* with seemingly impossible questions and we are both slack jaw when she throws one *Siri*'s way that *Siri* gets right. *Siri* is only going to get smarter!

Grads too may love *Siri*, but *Siri* and her decedents are going to be a major competitor for positions they may have qualified for during their lifetimes.

CURRENT JOB SEARCH STRATEGY IS "WING IT!"

So, we spent a few minutes evaluating how a globally talented market and highly functioning computers will continue to displace workers, and make it more and more difficult for your graduate to get a job.

Now, I want to open your eyes a bit to show you how far behind the eight ball your graduate is in starting to build his or her job search strategy. We'll take a look at just how little time, attention, focus and thought your student has put into the job search.

I've mentioned that it's taking the average grad 7.4 months to get a job after graduation a couple of times to keep driving home the point.

If you and your student start developing and managing a career strategy the minute he or she gets into college, there is a greater chance he or she will not only have a job by graduation day, but a job that is more relevant to your student's career and major.

Your incentive to help keep your student focused is the fact that he or she will have $3,000 to $4,000 in salary immediately after graduation.

It takes a commitment and time, but without you or the college or university requiring your student to invest the time, students will simply not put time into it. The end game and focus for your student will be on graduating.

Your student's first priority is the curriculum.

While in college, we estimate your child will invest up to 8 -10 thousand hours in class, creating reports, contributing to group projects, doing research, writing papers, preparing examples and being involved in campus activities. Add in down time, connecting with friends, some nights out, and holding down a job, and there is not a lot of time left.

To learn more about recent grads' job hunting strategies, TalentMarks conducted a series of polls several weeks after graduation in May, 2011. The results were disturbing:

- 60% of the grads surveyed spent 1-5 hours a week searching for a job.

- 17% spent 6-13 hours a week searching for a job.

- 95% of the grads did not have a written job career plan.

- 61% of the grads did not have an alumni mentor during college. 32% had one or two mentors.

These numbers showed graduates either didn't know the many different techniques to look for a job or were simply lazy. <u>My guess is their only knowledge about how to look for a job is to post some resumes on job boards, and wait for someone to contact them.</u>

RESEARCH CONFIRMS THEY DON'T USE MULTIPLE STRATEGIES!

The Heldrich study we mentioned in the second chapter, *Unfulfilled Expectations: Recent College Graduates Struggle in a Troubled Economy*, painted a picture about strategies used by the average graduate to get a job.

- Three-fifths of graduates use the Internet and job boards like Monster, CareerBuilder, and company websites.

- Three-fifths of graduates turned to family and friends.

- Less than 33% used their college career center.

Prior to 2007, while online job boards were emerging, the primary way to find a job was simply to look through classified ads in various publications and send resumes or call employers.

Having a good resume is only one of a dozen (or maybe more) skills in which your child will need to stand out in an uncertain job market. Today's students have to be adept at using online search techniques and social media, as well as master the skills involved in creating a resume that will be picked up because of focus on the right key words, building an online presence, networking skills, and understanding on how to build a job search strategy.

For the graduates of 2007 and those that came before, having a degree and a good resume was all they needed to get out and get interviews. Interviews and job offers came easily and most students didn't prepare, in fact, "winging it" was common.

Today's students can't wing it.

NO JOB SEARCH STRATEGY = POOR CAREER START!

Without the knowledge concerning how to look for a job or develop a job search plan prior to graduation – job seekers:

- get disillusioned.

- become frustrated.

- feel helpless and worthless.

- start to procrastinate.

- feel less confident.

- settle for less.

The Heldrich study found that 56% of the graduates feel -- based on the current market and world conditions -- that their earning potential will be less than that of their parents. Cliff Zukin, the co author of the Heldrich report, summarized what this generation is facing:

> "The dismal sense of college graduates' financial future is yet another sign of the corrosive effect of the Great Recession. Even young graduates of four-year colleges and universities, who are typically optimistic about their futures, are expressing doubt in another cornerstone of the American dream – that each generation can enjoy more prosperity than the one that came before it."

Man, just reading this bums me out!

Is this what you want for your graduate after all the time and investment both you and your student have made?

BUT WAIT! IT GETS WORSE!

Without the job skills necessary to get a job, students will find that they have fewer choices and because they have to support themselves, and they start to settle for whatever they can get. The Heldrich report proves this:

- 27% took a job just to get by and pay bills.

- 23% reported working for a temporary agency or doing seasonal work after graduation.

- 33% took a job that paid a lot less than they had anticipated after investing 4 years (or more) and tens of thousands of dollars in a college degree.

- 40% didn't think a college degree was necessary for the jobs they had.

If you think that is bad news, it starts to look even bleaker because research conducted by the National Bureau of Economic Research shows,

> "Graduating in a recession leads to large initial earnings losses. These losses, which amount to about 9 percent of annual earnings in the initial stage, eventually recede, but slowly -- halving within five years but not disappearing until about ten years after graduation."

Are you seeing the picture I'm trying to paint?

Your graduate cannot "wing it" and start developing his or her career management and job search strategies after graduation. There is plenty of evidence that your student will short change his or her opportunities and settle for jobs that are totally unrelated to his or her career goals, passions and dreams.

IS IT WORTH DEVELOPING A CAREER PLAN?

Yes!

A survey conducted by the National Association of Colleges and Employers, the association that your student's career centers belong to, found that graduating college seniors who used their school's career centers had a much greater chance of landing a job then those who didn't use the career center. The survey also found that students that used the career center more frequently than others had a higher chance of getting hired.

Of the students who participated in the study, 71 percent who got jobs had used the services of their schools' career centers. Further, those that visited more frequently received better salaries!

That research was complemented in the John J. Heldrich Center for Workforce Development report that found that:

- Students who had an internship received a median income of $6,680 more than those that did not do an internship.

- Those working during school in an area related to their major entered the labor force with a median income of $34,510; those not having done so entered with a median salary of $28,000.

- Graduates who were able to find a job that somehow related to the field in which they earned their college degree received a salary in their first job of $35,000, versus $25,000 for those that did not.

Throughout this book we'll be talking about strategies to help students explore career opportunities and develop a job search plan prior to graduation so they can be included in these positive statistics.

SUMMARY

The stakes are high for graduates and parents of this generation.

The end game for students is to get a great career job by graduation day. However, we've shared enough information and statistics to you that by now that you know better. The likelihood of finding a career-worthy job is small if your student doesn't have a plan.

Because the colleges and students are not focused on this, somebody has to be! I can't think of a better somebody than you and your student!

COMING UP

Why can't your student just go out there and figure it out? In the next chapter we'll share how much the job search process has changed and why students don't have a clue about how to look for a job in the 21st century.

Even as demand and salaries rise, college students should not be lulled into thinking that the job search will be easy or that jobs will be handed to anyone with a degree.

- John Challengers

YOUR TO DO'S AND NOTES!

CHAPTER RESOURCES

Visit Your College Career Center!

Parent Online Boot Camp & Parent Career Orientation Webinars
www.theunemployedgrad.com

If your student is graduating, or a recent grad, you should participate in the Parent Online Boot Camp! For parents whose students are entering, or in college check out the Parent Career Orientation Webinars!

JOB SEARCH & HIRING HAS DRAMATICALLY CHANGED

Your graduate needs traditional job search skills like networking, interviewing and the knowledge to build a fantastic resume, but he or she is also going to have to learn how to look for a job using online communities and social media.

When I entered my senior year of college the only thing on my mind was finishing up my courses required to graduate. As it was, on the last day of classes, and graduation the very next day, I found myself standing in front of my dean's desk asking him to wave an hour class I overlooked that would have prevented me from graduating.

My guess is there are a lot of students out there like me!

While in college I was active in as many clubs as I could be while working a full time, second shift job. I had a small part to play in producing the yearbook, and also had my own radio program on the campus radio station from 6:00 am– 8:00 am every day. I loved the responsibility of firing up the station, and being able to play a set of songs to wake up fellow students.

Upon graduation, it suddenly dawned on me that I didn't want to be a reporter, nor live the transient life of a disk jockey. Like most graduates today, I was fairly clueless about what to do, what industries I might work in, and/or how I could find positions within the entertainment or music industries.

I didn't have anyone to talk to about alternate directions for my career. It never dawned on me that I could go into the operations and management side of the radio business.

Had I talked to someone that could have offered advice on management, operations and other business areas I could have explored, I probably would not be writing this book. I would be near the end of a career that spanned working with Capital, Columbia, a cable company, or the new entertainment conglomerate Live Nation!

So what was my strategy? You guessed it-- "Wing it"!

I picked up the Cleveland Plain Dealer and started circling classified job listings for which I felt I was qualified. While writing this book, I ran across a copy of the resume I put together after graduating which included a listing of the part time jobs I held in college, my activities, and even my height and weight! (The theory that you gain 10 pounds every decade is true!) Obviously, I had not been to the career center for help!

I LEFT COLLEGE LOOKING OR A JOB - NOT A CAREER!

As a result of my "wing it" attitude, there was no strategic thought behind my job search, and my search quickly started to focus on the type of jobs where people called me back – sales jobs! It didn't seem that hard back then to get an interview because most of the sales positions were very low in base pay, with most salaries relying on commissions.

I did get a job within a couple weeks selling Pert and Perky note cards from Current Stationary, a firm out of the gorgeous Colorado Springs, Colorado area. My job found me moving from Ohio to Kansas City, Missouri to be a regional sales representative. Armed with the first business cards in my career, and I was responsible for visiting all the schools in the area and convincing kids to go out and sell Pert and Perky note cards.

In those days, we were able to walk into schools and knock on the doors of teachers --while they were teaching-- and try to pitch them. Today, if I did that in Kansas City, I'd be escorted from the front door by a Police officer, directly to the principal's office-- that is, after I was body searched and passed a metal detector!

Remember I said I was looking for a job, not a career. I quickly learned I didn't believe in my product, although any self respecting woman of the era thought very highly of Pert and Perky note cards. Within six months, I had fixed my resume, added my new responsibilities, picked up the classifieds, and started making phone calls.

That was then!

Today, your student is entering a world where the job search process has drastically changed, and the tools used to get a job are numerous and new.

And, the old standby-- the resume-- is about to become part of ancient history. The resume is about to go the way of the typewriter, cassette tape, land line phones, newspapers, and magazines.

This is a huge game changer as the entire job search process has been built on resumes and job postings.

Companies posted job listings and job seekers offered their resumes as proof they could do the jobs. It worked well until the Internet opened opportunities for anyone and everyone to blast 100 resumes to companies regardless of whether they were qualified for the positions for which they were applying. Hiring managers were overwhelmed with 250 or more resumes for each job and responded by developing software programs that looked for keywords in the resumes and which could eliminate 99 percent of them if they wanted to.

The process is changing because it's too time consuming, too expensive and too unpredictable!

3 EXAMPLES ON HOW THE JOB SEARCH PROCESS IS CHANGING

Before we look at the six primary reasons why job searching is changing, let me share 3 stories with you.

QUIZ/SURVEYS

In an article she wrote for the Wall Street Journal, Rachel Emma Silverman shared the changes in hiring techniques that John Fischer, founder and owner of StickerGiant.com, a Hygiene, Colorado company is already using. Fischer told Silverman that a resume isn't the best way to determine whether a potential employee will be a good social fit for the company. Instead his firm uses an online survey to help screen applicants.

The company designs questions tailored to the positions they need filled. For example a current opening for an Adobe Illustrator asks applicants about their skills, but also asks questions like "What is your ideal or dream job?", and "What is the best job you've ever had?"

The company provides applicants the option to attach a resume but it is not required. According to the founder, using quizzes like this are filtering techniques that can be automated so it saves the company time, yet produces a better match for the company. Keep in mind this is not a high tech or venture backed company! This is a middle of the road manufacturing company that is scrappy enough to know the old way is not working for them so they are using the new tools and techniques the internet provides them to speed up the process, reduce the costs, and make hiring more predictable.

SHORT TERM PAID PROJECTS

In another example of rejecting resumes, IGN Entertainment, a gaming and media firm launched a program in which it taught programming skills to passionate gamers that had little programming experience. They paid the participants while they learned. What they were looking for was a group of people with natural talent and the right attitude.

They used this as a way to sift through a bunch of candidates and to see firsthand how they worked.

Greg Silva, the Vice Present of People and Places for the firm indicated that out of the 30 participants who participated in the program, they eventually hired 6 people full time. Several of the candidates were not traditional candidates; they didn't attend college or have minimum work experience. If they had used resumes as part of the selection process, these people would have never been hired.

POWER POINTS AND TWEETS

Every day, we hear unique stories about how candidates are using new technology that bypasses traditional channels and tools like resumes to get jobs. One made an impression on me is a story about Hanna Phan, who was months into her job search using traditional job search techniques. Hanna was using social media and LinkedIn to build her network but she was not getting leads and worse - no interviews.

The good news was, she knew what she wanted to do. She wanted a job that combined technology and visual creative presentations. That's a pretty small niche!

Hanna did her research and noticed a job opening at SlideRocket, an online firm that makes presentation software. It looked like the kind of firm she could learn to love! Then, Hanna had an inspiration. She decided to use the company's own product to tell her story. Not a resume.

She created a 2 minute introduction to her accomplishments and goals using SlideRocket's technology. Think of it as an online, souped-up Power Point presentation.

She then tweeted her animated 90 second slide show to the company's chief executive, Chuck Dietrich. Many in upper management will share their Twitter accounts with the public because it not only builds social credibility and thought leadership but it's a less time consuming way to communicate with people.

At that very moment, Dietrich was settling into a flight heading west. He noticed a direct message from a Twitter follower named Hanna. Catching his curiosity, he clicked on the link and was impressed with the slideshow as well as Hanna's ingenuity in reaching out to him directly - using HIS product.

The CEO connected Hanna via phone when he landed, which led to a flight to the company's offices in San Francisco for an interview. Within a week, she had the job! The company put her resume on their website as an example of how their product can be used and, very quickly, it had 30,000 views! You can't do that with a resume.

Nobody else who applied for this job had a chance!

Incidentally, the company loved her application of their product so they produced a template slide share tool they call Presume, yet another tool your graduate should be looking at to make himself or herself look different.

If the principle service of your student's college is helping them with a resume, your student is going to graduate with little knowledge about how to survive in this changing world of Presumes, quizzes, surveys and companies who will try them out, before they hire them.

SIX PRIMARY CHANGES

There is a world of change happening in the job search industry brought on by six primary changes that are going to vastly affect your graduate's job search for the rest of his or her life!

<u>What we are starting to see is an entirely new job search process that will put more pressure and responsibility on the job seeker.</u> It's not going to get easier for most candidates. In fact, it will become more time consuming for them, unless they get ahead of this change and prepare.

Many of the changes have come over the past decade, with the real impact happening in only the last 4-5 years. So if you've been in your current job at least 5 years, you might be clueless about how much has changed too!

The changes that are occurring are primarily fueled by four things:

- Over supply of candidates applying for more jobs

- Technology

- Cost

- Global talent

In fact, one of the many challenges hiring managers have is trying to keep their recruitment costs down. According to the human-resources consulting firm Bersin & Associates, the cost to hire a new employee averages $3,479! Many larger firms are spending twice that amount. Cost control, efficiency, and technology are going to continue to drive changes in the recruitment, hiring and training processes.

Let's take a look at the six primary changes that have occurred over the past decade:

1. Job boards

2. Automated resume readers

3. Social Media

4. Online Community

5. New job search tools

6. Employment Checks

1) Job Boards

CareerBuilder was founded in 1994 and was one of the first online job posting sites that took advantage of the Internet. It was revolutionary at the time and in direct competition with the newspaper classified ads business.

Today CareerBuilder has over 23 million unique visitors per month. Others include SimplyHired, TheLadder, AfterCollege and Monster. There are literally tens of thousands of specialty job boards.

Job boards have come a long way and have essentially taken over a large part of the classified ads business. By 2008, revenue in the classified ads industry dropped by 42% from its peak that year. It's still a billion dollar industry, but it's no longer the only "game" in town.

Craigslist was founded in 1995 by Craig Newmark and served as centralized network of online communities in specific cities that provides free classified advertising with sections devoted to jobs, housing personals, for sale, and more.

Not only were job boards less expensive, faster, and easier for companies to participate in, but they gave employers access to a nationwide audience.

Job boards also provided new benefits for job seekers. They could post their resume information online which eliminated the need to print it out, including the cover letter, or put postage on it and mail it.

A number of companies have developed techniques where a person can fill in one resume online, push a button, and apply automatically in hundreds of jobs. This Gatling gun technique rarely works, but the ease and low cost nature of the service is hard for job seekers to pass up.

Unfortunately, this put new burdens on hiring managers. Instead of having to review 10-20 paper resumes, they were now being bombarded with hundreds of electronic resumes. Plus, they had to shift through the resumes to attempt to look for lies, exaggerations and distortions of truth.

Let's step into the shoes of a hiring manager for a quick second.

Let's assume they have received 250 resumes for a position. Their crafty little program will sort through and per their instructions find 50 that match the keyword criteria that the manager is looking for. From that point:

- They will probably call the top 15 to 20

- Once they talk to the above candidates, they will probably check 3-7 of the candidates' online identities.

- Then, they will likely bring in the top 3 candidates

The odds are definitely against your student being called in for an interview, let alone him or her getting the job.

The Internet and an explosion of new techniques have actually made hiring managers' jobs harder, not easier. When your student applied to college, he or she probably participated in common application systems where they only had to fill in one college application and they could use it at participating colleges. Today, your student's resume represents only $1/20^{th}$ of the overall strategy about how to get a job. He or she has to stand out in order to be chosen.

2) Automated resume readers

With the introduction of job boards and a flood of new resumes, hiring managers needed a secret weapon to offload the piles of ridiculously unqualified people who were electronically applying for everything under the sun.

So programmers gave them an easy to use tool that is tied together with the job description of the position and which will automatically scan electronically submitted resumes, grade them, and kick out the best matches to the hiring manager.

This program will look for keywords or key phrases in the resume. Each system is different and most give the hiring manager the ability to weigh certain phrases. The job seeker's challenge is to find repetitive words in the job description and try to load their resume with similar words in order for the computer program to include them in the final selection offered to the hiring manager.

As computers and programs become more sophisticated, there are changes on the horizon that will use semantic matching programs to even more accurately match a person to a position. Smarter technology uses advanced algorithms to find the best matches automatically or drill down with pinpoint semantic searches that far exceed the compatiblities of traditional full text search engines.

With this innovation, job seekers now need to take some time to evaluate the keywords in the job description and reword a resume to include those. It's more time consuming and of course, every time you tinker with your resume there is a good chance you will misspell something.

The good news is resume readers are used primarily by larger companies. If your student is not interested in working for a large company, this will be less of a headache and time killer for him or her. Ninety-nine percent of employers in the U.S. are small businesses with less than 16 employees. They don't typically have the same volume of resumes for a position, nor the access to filtering technologies.

However, that is changing.

Companies like Unrabble provide easy to read resume tools for small and medium sized businesses for as little as $29 per month for a company. Their tool can pull in candidates and give the hiring manager a dashboard on which they can change the parameters to specify what they are looking for.

This program can even confirm the person's employment, Google a name, send out questions for written responses, and automatically update everyone involved in hiring for the position. It's pretty neat stuff as it helps hiring managers go through the hiring process faster, with less hassle and/organizes the relevant information they and others need to make selections. It eliminates a lot of the start/stop situations that typically occur during the hiring process.

I know we've been talking about the death of resumes, but in no way are we saying to abandon resumes altogether.

We live between times right now and your student still needs a resume!

We highly recommend your student use the career center to help them develop a resume, as well as read books and publications, or even attend webinars to learn more about the resume process.

3) Social Media

Social media has made an enormous impact on how companies are looking for employees and how employees find job opportunities over the last couple of years.

Social media for job searching and hiring is relatively new. Social media has been acknowledged as starting around 2004 with a series of new websites that enabled people to interact with each other and content for those sites was created. Some of the first that you are familiar with today include MySpace, Flickr, Twitter, YouTube and blogs.

Social media can be used to find jobs but also help candidates do something they never could do before – be found. That's an interesting opportunity because a candidate is going to be in a stronger position to get a job IF the hiring manager seeks him or her out.

Let's take a look at the most popular Social Media job search tools.

Twitter

When Renee Libby, 25, was laid off from her public relations position she decided to see if Twitter might help her get a job.

She started searching on Twitter for local communication professionals in the Baltimore area. Once she found them, she simply connected with them. This gave her a chance to build a network of Directors of Communications, Marketing and even VP's. While connecting with others, she made sure her Twitter page showed her experience, and to keep in front of her new contacts, she Tweeted regularly.

Every hour or so, Renee would tweet about news or articles specific to the industries in Baltimore or send out links to the latest edition of her own column in a local publication. In what would seem lightening speed time for others who are in the job search process, the Director of Public Relations for Baltimore-based SPIN contacted Libby and suggested she start freelancing for the company, which she gladly did.

As with anything, timing is everything. Only one week later, one of their associates announced that she was leaving. That left Renee with an inside track at interviewing for the position, which she eventually got!

Twitter, with now one hundred and forty million users, represents another network that hiring managers are using because it's fast, effective and free! They can post a job and within seconds start receiving responses from people.

There are four ways to use Twitter to get jobs.

Your student is going to have to become a savvy Twitter user. It could be the differentiator that helps him or her stand out.

- Make comments and post on company Twitter accounts or Twitter accounts of people within the companies he or she is interested in working for.

- Create a Twitter account to show thought leadership.

- Build a personal brand.

- Subscribe to Twitter accounts that list job opportunities.

Your student should create his or he own Twitter account --not only to allow to follow companies he or she is interested in and receive these alerts-- but also to show his or her own thought leadership. If your student is interested in sustainable management, and continually tweets or re-tweets a company's message, tracking tools will show the company that your student is helping get its message out. When it comes time to hire, your student's name will be familiar.

Another reason your student should create a Twitter account and build his or her connections on Twitter is to help get the message out when he or she needs a job. There are thousands of stories already of individuals who tweeted something like, "Just got laid off, looking for work in accounting – small business" and then instantly getting leads from people who followed them or follow their followers!

YouTube

We are big advocates of video. It's the new way to stand out because most people are not using video effectively. We recommend your student create a video that gives a 1-2 minute overview of their accomplishments, awards, goals and what they bring to the table of a company. With a flip-it camera or even a smart phone, your student can record an interview, edit it, add transitions and graphics to make it look professional, and maybe even include some music on the front and back ends.

This video can be used on a personal page, linked to their LinkedIn and/or Facebook pages, and posted on YouTube. YouTube has hundreds of millions of users that search its contents every day. Having a video on YouTube will draw more attention to your student and it will also show up when a company is doing an online check-up on him or her. It's just another way to look innovative, professional and relevant in these times.

Blogs

There are four ways to use blogs to get jobs.

- Make comments and post on company blogs or the blogs of people within the company.

- Create a blog to show thought leadership.

- Subscribe to blogs that list job opportunities.

- Build a personal brand.

Blogging started to become popular in 2004 as free tools like Wordpress and Typepad were introduced, and today it's pretty mainstream. Most companies and a select number of their employees are now blogging.

Your student is going to want to isolate the companies they really want to work for and then search for the company and/or individuals who work on the company's blog. He or she can do that on Technorati, a website that catalogs over 125 million blogs. When your student finds the company and/or individuals within the company, he or she can use tools like Google News or RSS Feeds to alert them when new posts are made. Then, if it's appropriate, they can drop in and make comments and/or share the posts with the network. Again this is all about getting noticed within the company.

There are thousands of niche blogs that list job opportunities. Mashable is one of the best known technology blogs in the industry. (nearly 900,000 people have "liked" it) Mashable realized another way they could monetize their blog was to list jobs. So while browsing an article, readers can pop over and instantly drop into Mashable's job listings.

The other way your student will want to use blogs is to build his or her own personal brand.

My kids have been developing blogs the over the last 4 years as a way to share their interests, skills, and knowledge. The two oldest have gone through a number of different blogs in search of what their brand should be. The best thing they did was just getting a blog started.

As their focus and interests have changed, they have moved onto different messages and entirely new blogs. April had at least 3 different blogs before she became focused on sustainability management. Now completing her degree in Sustainable Management with the University of Wisconsin, she decided to create a blog called, "Sustainably Small." She covers topics related to companies that are successfully implementing strategies that are green.

Along the way she learned about other blogs. One in particular was www.lagreengirl.com. She reached out to the founder of the blog and offered to periodically create guest blogs. She was turned down initially, but as the author saw April pick up on her own blog and liked what she was doing, she agreed. So April started covering events that the founder of LAGreenGirl could not cover.

That led to an opportunity for April to go to Costa Rica with company officials of Whole Foods to cover their natural foods strategy and blog about it. She spent a week with company officials visiting banana plantations, and learning how the company was practicing sustainable management in banana farming.

It all started with a blog, developing her own personal brand, and putting herself out to do things for others, and not expecting anything in return. I have reminded April that she will break the heart of all those communication and journalism majors from Ivy League, to state or private colleges who labored for four years to prepare themselves for opportunities like these.

Yet because April showed initiative, and was in the right place at the right time, she got the opportunity – even though she didn't carry a degree in communication/journalism or formal writing training for that matter!

My son Ben has been doing the same thing. Ben's on his second blog, and the latest writings are focused on marketing strategies. Now 8 months out of college, he's got a better feel for what turns him on in the business world, and he's anxious to share what he's learning and his ideas with others. I'm confident that given time, Ben will see career boosts from the time and investment he's making in his blog.

If it works for my family, it will work for yours!

4) Online Community

In 1996, I created an online community for college students called StudentAccess.com. Our target audience was college students and we gave them a free home page, email and the ability to post photographs. After spending about $20,000 marketing it to college students nationwide, we waited, waited, and waited-- and nothing happened.

Then all of a sudden our small server was reaching its maximum capacity. We thought it had finally caught on. Unfortunately, it wasn't college students on our site. It was pornographers who found our free home pages a great way to share their photographs.

We ended up closing the site down and went on to build online communities from 1996-2007 for alumni associations. By 2005, it appeared to me that either MySpace or Facebook was going to become the dominant online community. So I sold the firm to a competitor.

Today there are thousands of niche online communities that cater to organizations, interests and whims of just about everything under the sun. Recruiters are recognizing online communities are excellent places to find "stand out" people, people who show a great deal of interest, passion and expertise in their areas of interest.

Here's a good example.

In an article in the New York Times the Director of Talent Acquisition at Quicken Loans, shared how his company uses sometimes unorthodox methods to find quality people. They like to find people who are in the field and currently working and watch them in action. For the hiring manager, this cuts through the interviewing crap and gives him or her a real, live glimpse at the character of the person. The company once conducted a "blitz of local retail stores and restaurants, by sending employees out to interact with workers and to offer interviews to people who really stood out".

They have also been known to frequent online communities related to their industry and look for people that have what it takes to make it in the positions they are looking to hire. If a position comes up in their firm, they'll use search engines to find forums, online communities, and blogs that relate to that position and then hunker down and start watching and engaging. When they see someone that fits the description they are looking for, that person gets invited for an interview.

According to the 2011 Jobvite survey on corporate use of Internet strategies, 89 percent of companies intended to use candidates' social networks to source, recruit and check out candidates, which increased from 83 percent the year before. It also showed that:

- 64% had successfully hired people through social networks.

- 55% intended to invest more time and resources in social recruiting.

Ironically, the same report is showing that while company recruiters are adopting these methods to find quality people faster and with less hassle and cost, candidates are not using them as effectively as they could be.

Your student will need a strategy about how to professionally use these online communities. Let's take a look at the most important online communities that have already proven to help people get jobs.

Facebook

I like to remind how incredibly remarkable Facebook's growth has been by comparing it to the New York Times. Founded in 1848, the New York Times today has a little over one million subscribers. Facebook, founded in 2004, is today closing in on 1 BILLION subscribers and about to launch the biggest IPO in the history of the WORLD. It's a big deal!

It has become a communication, entertainment, news and personal networking hub that is sucking an average of one hour a day from consumers. But it is also becoming a powerful job search tool.

Here's proof!

The same survey mentioned by Jobvite found that more than 22 million members of the U.S. workforce found their most recent positions through social media (including online communities), up 7.7 million from the previous year.

Wow! That's a huge number!

Focusing on Facebook, the survey also found that:

- 86 percent of job seekers have social media profiles, with Facebook leading the pack at 84 percent, and 31 percent having profiles on Facebook, Twitter, and LinkedIn.

- More than one-third of job seekers with Facebook profiles do not use that social network as part of their job search in any way, unlike nearly all of those with LinkedIn profiles and three-quarters of those on Twitter.

- 48 percent of all job seekers, and 63 percent of those with Facebook profiles, have used the social network for at least one activity related to job hunting over the past year.

- One out of five job seekers added their professional information to their Facebook profiles during the past year.

- 18 percent of job seekers received job referrals from Facebook friends.

Jobvite's survey suggests that 18.4 million Americans said Facebook was the source that led to their current positions. Employers are getting hip. Employers will go where prospective employees are. At the time I'm writing this book, there are 76 million U.S. Facebook users under 30 years old, versus 5.5 million on LinkedIn.

Depending on the industry in which your student is seeking a job, Facebook will continue to increase in importance as a way for your student to network with others and look for jobs.

LinkedIn

LinkedIn was founded by Reid Hoffman the same year as Facebook and MySpace and is now the dominate business networking online community with over 160,000,000 million users, a number that is growing. Its professional focus has limited its growth, but its business networking capacity is becoming more and more important for anyone wanting to do business or get a job.

LinkedIn is becoming the de facto replacement for a resume. It provides more information than a resume and can be scanned and shared by a group of people responsible for hiring a student. It includes

- Photo

- Summary of experience

- Awards

- Details of work experience

- Links to blogs, twitter and online personal sites

- Recommendations/Testimonials

- Ability to share projects, power points, etc.

- Skills

To make it even easier for employers and prospective employees, LinkedIn introduced an "apply now" button on its job postings that sends the data in a job seeker's profile directly to a potential employer.

Employers are taking notice and using LinkedIn more. In a study by Jobvite, it was found that 73 percent of all hires made through social networks were via LinkedIn and 41 percent of employee referrals for jobs involved LinkedIn. <u>Few students and graduates are skilled at using LinkedIn, but it's clear they are going to need to get up to speed - fast!</u>

Google +

Google has re-launched an online community which in less than a year will reach 150 million users.

Google + provides a similar online community experience as that Facebook provides but they integrate all of their products and services into it. I'm not confident that Google + will become as popular and used as Facebook, but I do see it becoming a powerful new tool for groups and organizations to work on projects. I see a time when your student will be working with a career coach online in what is called "Hangouts"-- online video chat rooms.

Niche Communities

The behaviors of consumers have changed in the last 5 years so that online communities are part of their daily habits and we expect these consumers to become even more active as companies integrate products and services with them via television/cable, cell phones and other devices.

There are hundreds of thousands of niche communities in which your student could participate that relate to their career goals and interests. Niche communities might be an online community of accountants in Ohio, paleontologists in Europe or health and fitness experts globally. A growing number of organizations and many companies are developing their own online communities to engage and connect with others. If your student knows the niche he or she is interested in, many times smaller online communities will give him or her more of an opportunity to be noticed.

Did we make our point?

<u>Your student's job search will more than likely involve online communities</u>. There is a culture and there are emerging acceptable norms associated with each of the new channels. They will need to be aware of how to "play" within these environments.

5) Employment Checks

We live in more complicated times today than ever before. Over the decades we've all heard about child molesters working within schools, drug addicts working in hospitals, criminals working in the financial industry. The good news about these stories is they have forced organizations to be responsible to check on prospective employees' backgrounds before they are hired.

This process not only protects consumers, but it can also prevent qualified candidates from getting jobs when the things that turn up are not-- or should not-- be part of the hiring managers concerns.

The vast majority of small business employers do not do extensive background checks, but the technology and the effort to do so continues to get less expensive and easier to adopt, so we anticipate seeing more organizations doing employment checks in the future.

These checks, for whatever reason, can throw your student out of the running. It might be misstating information on the dates of their employment; it might be information that comes up in a credit and/ or criminal check.

The times we live in are requiring organizations to look beyond the resume and verify background information like:

- Driving records

- Vehicle registration

- Credit records

- Criminal records

- Social Security no.

- Education records

- Court records

- Workers' compensation

- Bankruptcy

- Character references

- Neighbor interviews

- Medical records

- Property ownership

- Military records

- State licensing records

- Drug test records

- Past employers

- Personal references

- Incarceration records

- Sex offender lists

Whew! That's quite a list.

But that's not all!

The Fair Consumer Reporting Act even allows background checks that can include interviews with "neighbors, friends, or associates" about your "character, general reputation, personal characteristics, or mode of living"

Background reports can range from a verification of an applicant's Social Security number to a detailed account of the potential employee's history and acquaintances.

There is even some evidence that employers are now searching popular social networking Web sites such as MySpace and Facebook for the profiles of applicants. An October 2007 survey from Vault.com found that 44% of employers use social networking sites to obtain information about job applicants, while 39% have searched such sites for information about current employees. Your student needs to be reminded that his or her online life will be a part of the employment check.

If your student anticipates working for a large firm, having a poor credit rating could knock him or her out of the running for a job. A good friend of mine's son applied for an entry level job at Nationwide Insurance. By entry level, I mean they required a college degree and a clean credit report for a starting salary under $35,000. Fortunately he was a great kid, good grades and good credit rating, so he got the job!

I'd recommend that your student pay attention to one of the zillion ads on TV for FreeCreditScore.com and check out his or her credit rating as soon as possible. If there is anything on their credit that could affect a hiring position, he or she may have time to correct it.

There is more!

Research is showing that a large percentage of resumes are filled with lies, distortions and exaggerations of responsibilities. Hiring managers are tasked with uncovering fact and fiction, and they do!

According to research conducted by The Society of Human Resource Managers, over 53% of individuals lie about on resumes in some way. Lying on resumes is becoming more, and more common. When college students were asked in the same study, over 70% said they would lie on their resumes to land their dream job.

So what do they lie about?

According to the CareerBuilder.com survey, these were the most common falsehoods told on a resume:

- 38 percent of those surveyed indicated they had embellished their job responsibilities.

- 18 percent admitted to lying about their skill set.

- 12 percent indicated they had been dishonest about their start and end dates of employment .

- 10 percent confessed to lying about an academic degree.

- 7 percent said they had lied about the companies they had worked for.

- 5 percent disclosed that they had been untruthful about their job title.

That puts even more responsibility on companies to do their "due diligence" and conduct a "truth test" of the resumes. Most companies don't have the time to ferret these out so they outsource it to third parties who do a very thorough job.

I was helping a local manufacturer select a sales manager for a brand new position and did the initial sort through of the 75 resumes received. After I narrowed it down to 7 people and held phone interviews, I eliminated 4 and had 3 to present to management. The one candidate I selected as the frontrunner didn't initially click with the president of the firm and he picked my third choice candidate, so it looked like a done deal.

However, within a week, the firm that did the background check came back with big red flags on the candidate's past employment history. I have to say, the person interviewed had an impressive background but his resume check knocked him out of the position. The firm hired the person I initially recommended and they are still working together 5 years later.

You have to put yourself in the position of the hiring manager and while you want your student to "look good," you must be careful about how far you advise them to go to show off their accomplishments, because hiring managers will be asking these questions:

- **Job title/Role:** Is the title inflated? How many directors can one company have?

- **Job Requirements:** Do the responsibilities match the role? Are they embellished?

- **Financial Success**: Has the candidate exaggerated on the revenue brought in or financial benefits to make himself or herself appear more successful?

- **Dates of Employment:** Are they accurate? Have they been tampered with to remove gaps of unemployment?

- **Certification or degree:** Did the candidate complete, fail, or drop out? Was the degree listed attained? Can this be confirmed?

- **Previous salary**: Does the salary mach the role and responsibilities? Check W-2 history.

- **Reason for leaving previous employer**: Does the wording mask poor performance, or a conflict situation?

- **Academic dates**: Has the candidate changed these to cover failed or repeated subjects?

- **Technical abilities:** Is the candidate exaggerating? Does the candidate really understand ASP.NET?

Keep in mind, your student may be an excellent candidate but ANY of the issues listed above could keep him or her from ever seeing a hiring manager at a company.

6) New job search tools

Along with online communities and social media, a new crop of tools has been developed to help people get noticed in a crowded job market. Your student should be familiar with these tools because they work.

I know, as my son has had firsthand experience with one in particular. Like most grads he spent some time looking for jobs while in college, but not enough to have a job on graduation day. After moving home, he saw an opportunity for an internship with a high end web development and marketing company in Santa Monica. Except for being an internship with a low hourly pay, it sounded like the kind of company he wanted to work for. The internship had been listed for 3 months and it was scheduled to start in just 3 weeks.

Instead of applying for the position, Ben sent a video email that introduced himself to the company. Before he sent the email, he spent time reviewing the company mission, vision and goals and incorporated in his intro his understanding of what they needed to do and how he could help them achieve it. The next morning he received an email from the hiring manager that said, "When can you start?"

I said it before, and I'll say it again here, "If it works for my kids, it will work for your kids!"

Other interesting tools include:

- JobTacToe
- RezScore
- InterviewStream
- Video Bio
- Reach

JobTacToe

I love this tool because it makes a game out of looking for a job and provides encouragement along the way. JobTacToe is an online tool founded by a group of smart Harvard grads that wanted to help job seekers not feel so isolated and alone during the job search and at the same time offer continual suggestions on how they could get jobs. It's a fascinating free tool available to anyone today,

RezScore

RezScore will enable your student to see if their resume has the stuff to get noticed. It will not only find spelling errors but it will look for relevancy and missing components that could get him or her thrown out of a job search process.

InterviewStream

Few graduates realize how hard it is to get to the interview process. We've talked at length about changes that have occurred in the job search process and yet, the interview process is pretty much the same as it always has been – except few people learn how to interview, or spend any time practicing. Interview Stream will give your student the ability to interview online.

Video Bio

We like to remind students that they need an arsenal of tools and techniques to keep themselves in front of hiring managers. That's why we recommend they use social media and online communities. Video Bio provides a way for them to create their own personal video bio that can be sent to hiring managers. It's a great way for hiring managers to see how articulate and professional your student can be.

360 Reach

I also love this tool. Reach has a tool that allows your student to build his or her own personal brand. Your student goes to the website, enters the email addresses of people they'd like to get feedback from and then those targeted people will be asked to describe your student. All responses are confidential. Your student gets back anonymous responses of what people see in him or her. While your student may feel insecure and not confident, others may see him or her as a risk taker, innovative and passionate. The responses will give your student a better idea of how others perceive him or her so he or she can continue to embellish those traits or add behaviors that will influence others opinions of him or her.

These are only a few of the hundreds of new emerging tools available that will help your student get a job.

SUMMARY

Whew!

We covered a lot in this chapter but did so to bring to your attention the TREMENDOUS changes that have occurred in the personal career management and job search process.

Never in the history of our country have so many changes, happened so fast for both the job seeker and hiring manager. Those that understand these changes and embrace them will succeed. Those that don't will struggle, end up frustrated and have lose out on great candidate or job opportunities.

Your student's formal education is soon to end, but he or she now needs to focus for the rest of his or her life on managing a career!

COMING UP!

Your student is going to need to have an online identity in order to stand out and get jobs.   We'll look at how he or she can create a professional online identity.

Do not follow where the path may lead. Go, instead, where there is no path and leave a trail.

- Ralph Waldo Emerson

YOUR TO DO'S AND NOTES!

_____

_____

_____

_____

_____

_____

_____

_____

_____

_____

CHAPTER RESOURCES

Visit Your College Career Center!

Grad Career Toolkit

www.theunemployedgrad.com

You can give your graduate access to the essential Grad Career Toolkit that will include over 40 ideas, tips and tools that will help them get a job! Free!

AN ONLINE IDENTITY TRUMPS RESUMES!

Your student has no idea the role their online identity is going to play in their ability to move from job to job with fewer negative effects and less anxiety.

How much time do you think hiring managers spend looking at resumes?

A study conducted by The Ladders wanted to see if the self reported time of approximately 4 minutes per resume was accurate.

They set up an extensive analysis that watched how long recruiters spent looking at resumes; how quickly their eyes moved from item to item and what content was overlooked. Using eye tracking technology gave them a scientific way to document the resume review process. Their process showed that 80 percent of the time hiring managers reviewed a resume, they focused on the candidates:

- Name
- Current title/company
- Previous title/company
- Previous position's start and end dates

- Current positions start and end dates,

- Education.

- And the time to accomplish all that?

- Six seconds! Imagine that.

Picture for a moment your graduate's resume sitting in a stack of other resumes in front of a hiring manager. The hiring manager has one thing on his/her mind. Get through the stack and narrow it down to 6-9 candidates for initial interviews. While the odds are better than the lottery, there is a great deal of luck associated with your grad's resume making the short list.

All the work, time and effort your graduate put into their college experience will be summarized in just six seconds by a hiring manager!

Hiring managers don't like this process either. They are looking for better ways to help them find the best candidates quicker, without having to try to guess from a piece of paper if a person qualifies for a position.

Union Square is a New York venture capital firm that invested in Twitter, Foursquare, and Zynga is doing just that!

They posted an opening for an investment analyst and instead of asking for resumes, the company asked applicants to send links representing their "Web presence," such as Twitter account or Tumblr blog. The firm says this process provides them better-quality candidates, and it shows them if the candidates have the kind of "thought leadership" and online presence they are looking for.

Union Square is not the only company moving in this direction.

Your student's online presence and identity is rapidly becoming MORE important than his or her resume. An online identity is the sum of your student's participation in online communities and social media. Through his or her participation, postings, and connections your student is creating a digital expression of identity.

This online identity started the minute you child began exploring the Internet.

As he or she enters the college years, your student needs to be thinking of who is looking at his or her participation, postings, and connections. While it's fine to post zany photos on Facebook & Twitter accounts as long as your student is controlling who sees them, he or she needs to be developing a professional side of himself or herself online at the same time!

An online identify is something your student can start his or her freshman year and continue to develop and modify. It's free, and requires only a few minutes a week. It really, really, *really* is going to be an important part of their job search, if not the differentiator he or she needs to not only get a job, but get the job he or she *wants*.

In order for you to be of any help in discussions with your child in this area, we'll spend some time in this chapter giving you an overview of the tools, services and how your student should be using them.

BUSINESS IS DRIVING THIS CHANGE!

This dramatic change in the job search process is not being driven by job seekers or students, its being driven by hiring managers around the world, because in many cases it's faster and less expensive than traditional job posting channels.

It's not unusual for large corporations/Fortune 500 companies to spend $1.2 million dollars a year to post employment opportunities on job boards. To post the same jobs on LinkedIn it would cost only $60,000. Or, if they were posting the same jobs on Twitter, the cost would drop to $8,000 or less!

> Remember, hiring managers look at each candidate they hire with trepidation. They don't want to make a mistake that will reflect poorly on them and their companies so they take their time in the hiring process. When a person comes recommended from someone from within the ranks of the company, that person carries more credibility as the employee is vouching the recommendation will be a good addition to the team. Social media and online communities foster this accepted and preferred practice with less effort.

For candidates, if properly done, using social media will help them get a job faster, with less effort because they are using the viral nature of the Internet to keep their networks aware of their capabilities and current status.

If done right, a social media hiring campaign has the potential to make it easier for the hiring manager to do his or her job!

DON'T BELIEVE IT?

Never in the history of human resources have new techniques been adopted as fast as these techniques are today. More importantly, using these hiring processes are rapidly becoming an engrained tool and behavior of hiring managers.

Consider these stats by Career Enlightenment, a resource website for job seekers. Their survey found that:

- 89% of US companies will use social networks for recruiting next year.

- Over 80% of companies will check a candidate's online profile in some way before hiring him or her.

- 14.4 million people used social media to find a job in 2011

- 79 percent of hiring managers and job recruiters review applicants' online information.

- 56 percent of hiring managers use networking sites to source prospective candidates. (This is up 54% from just 3 years ago.)

- 55% of companies surveyed indicated they planned to invest more in social recruiting in 2011.

- 80 percent indicated they used LinkedIn to find talent.

- 45 percent indicated they used Twitter to find talent.

While there are many upsides, there are a few downsides your student needs to be cognizant of:

- One out of three employers surveyed rejected a candidate because of what they found on a social media site.

- Over 2,000 people on LinkedIn have the same name as a person wanted on the FBI's most wanted list.

- Have I convinced you yet?

- Let's take a look at the fundamental tools your student should master if they want to have a successful career.

Your student's basic online strategy should include:

- A personal website

- LinkedIn profile

- Twitter account

- Facebook page

So let's look at how we can get your student up to speed and make sure they have some of the basics for creating a powerful social media job search strategy.

1) Personal Website

You might consider Facebook a personal website, but it doesn't have the flexibility your student can get by creating a website and modifying it. A personal website would give your student the ability to show his or her personal and professional life the way they want to.

Your student can:

- Show PowerPoint presentations of projects.

- Offer spreadsheets they completed for courses.

- Display portfolios of art and designs.

- Offer word documents of reports, articles and assignments.

- Post recommendations from faculty, staff and others.

- Include only photos he or she wants others to see.

- Post a video introduction and a bio of himself or herself.

There are a couple different ways to accomplish this.

A personal website can be built around free and easy to use blog software provided by WordPress and Blogger. Another option is to use companies like www.godaddy.com, www.1&1.com and www.homestead.com which have easy to use tools to set up a website and enable your student to buy a personal URL. For example if your student is Jonathon Jones Mellencamp, there is a good chance he can get JonathonJonesMellencamp.com, which is kind of cool and easy for others to remember.

I'd suggest your student include awards he or she received, certificates of achievement and definitely a digital image of his or her diploma. Showing a diploma will help your student stand out from others.

Like other strategies, your student will need to continually update, change and modify the website to keep it relevant to their jobs and responsibilities.

2) LinkedIn

LinkedIn was founded in 2004 and has become the online business networking site for people around the world.

At the time I published this book, LinkedIn had over 160 million professionals who used it as a way to build a personal and professional network. If you are in business, you need to be building your network here too!

I'm currently connected to over 1,200 people and am a member of 50 groups which give me access to over 13,000,000 business professionals. It's a pretty vast online rolodex that instantly gives me a shot at reaching the right people with whom to work on projects.

There are books written about how to use LinkedIn and many cover unique angles on how to use this resource. In our limited time and space together here, I'd like to share eight important things your student should be doing right now:

- Build out his or her profile page.

- Start connecting with alumni, then friends, classmates, family etc.

- Join 50 groups!

- Follow companies he or she is interested in.

- Participate in *Answers*.

- Share industry news and information.

- Get recommendations.

- Search for jobs.

Career centers are encouraging their seniors to create their LinkedIn accounts their senior year, but we'd like to reinforce that they need get it started their freshman years.

Let's take a look at each of these.

a) Build out their profile page

LinkedIn is not Facebook!

Your student needs to know there is a different culture and acceptable norms that have been established within the LinkedIn community. To begin with, your student should be using a professional photograph in which he or she is donning professional attire. For men, a tie or at least a sports coat, - no Hoodies! And for ladies, a nice blouse, sweater or even business suit is appropriate.

If your student's name is common, he or she might want to consider using a middle name. A quick search for John Smith produced over 34,000 results. Your student wants to make sure he or she can be found.

Along with a photo, the title line is very important because it's part of the information that LinkedIn indexes and outputs in search results. In other words, by putting in the right keywords or phrases, your student will show up more frequently when people are looking for someone with his or her capabilities and interests!

Here are a couple ideas on title lines:

- "Name of College graduate" with "Name of Major"- leadership experience

- I'm passionate about sales now that I have my degree from "Name of College."

- Need a dependable team player from "Name of College"? Call me!

Once yours students gets his or her first job, he or she might provide a summary of its duties:

- Project management assistant that keeps all project under budget and on time

- Systems engineer with deep understanding of C + and dot net nuke

- Marketing assistant with major focus on Social Media strategies

Your student can change the title line periodically to find one that provides the best results or to match current job responsibilities.

The profile page provides an assortment of information your student can share his or her professional skills, experience, accomplishments and knowledge.

For example, he or she can include:

- Terms that identify him or her

- Awards and recognitions

- Links to their Twitter and/or personal accounts

- Power Points and/or documents.

LinkedIn encourages everyone to fill in their profiles, and even reminds users when they are 50 percent, 80 percent and/or 100 percent complete. Even after they have finished their profiles, students should continually update them. One way they can do that is by integrating their blogs with their LinkedIn accounts so every time they publish articles on their blogs, they are automatically updated on their LinkedIn pages.

b) Start connecting with alumni, then friends, classmates, family etc.

I think the role of every alumni association is to connect students during their freshman years with a minimum of 5 alumni who are committed to staying in touch with the students. Mentors offer advice and even provide "virtual job shadowing. " Alumni associations or career centers try to encourage this but, because it is not required, few students do it.

It's really simple to connect to alumni.

All your student has to do is conduct a search for people from his or her college. After reviewing some of the contacts, he or she can simply ask to connect with them, and then after exchanging a few emails, your student can decide if he or she wants to develop a more formal networking and/or mentoring relationship.

In my opinion, your student should have connected with at least 50 alumni by the time he or she graduates.

Why?

Well, if they are connecting with alumni during their freshman and sophomore years, students will have other avenues to explore internships. Alumni will be more than willing to go an extra mile to help young alumni when they need it. Then, by the time they are graduating, these students can put their networks to work for them to help find jobs. I'm convinced that the more alumni they are connected to, the quicker they will get jobs, <u>and not just any jobs, jobs in their fields with higher salaries.</u>

Students need to keep in mind that mentoring is a two-way street. They will keep their mentors more engaged and active if they periodically connect with them, and give them an update on campus events and activities, inviting them to homecoming and/or asking them to share memorable moments they had while on campus. Your student needs to let the mentor share a part of who he or she is in addition to sharing career information. Bonding happens when people feel they've shared personal experiences and feelings.

Now at the same time students are connecting with alumni, they should be doing searches for people within the industries they are interested in and asking if they can connect with them too! During college is the best time to reach out to a Vice President or President of a company. Once your student is part of the working world, it may not be as easy to get connected to people in higher positions as he or she might assume it will –your student will be considered someone trying to sell these industry insiders a product or service. However, when an industry insider gets a request from a student that says, "I'm XXX from XXXX college and I started to do research on XXX industry and your name came up, I was hoping I could add you to my professional network and connect from time to time," he or she is more likely to be impressed.

Finally, make sure your student is connecting with you, your friends, members of your congregation, the organizations you belong to, etc.

c) Join 50 groups!

LinkedIn offers anyone or any group the opportunity to create a group around their interests, hobbies or organization. Alumni associations create them, people that work within specific industries create them, people in geographical areas create them. There are hundreds of thousands of groups.

There is one major benefit of joining groups that few people realize. When the person your student wants to network with is a member of the same group, your student can ask them to become a connection. If this isn't the case, your student has to ask a person they are connected to – that is, in turn, connected to that person- to connect (a time consuming process). If they don't take that route, they'll need to have the person's email address or have attended the same college.

Here's another tip:

> While I am a member of a few small groups (under 500 in size), I tend to join groups within my areas of interest that are the largest. Some have over 100,000 members. The reason your student wants to join the larger groups is that he or she will be able to directly connect with all 100,000 people in the group! It makes it easier for your student to build a network.

Groups are cool. They have:

- Discussion areas where anyone can bring up a topic for discussion and others can chime in on it. I've started discussions that had over 100 people offer their opinions and have gone on for months

- Promotional areas where organizations or individuals can offer services, related to the group.

- Member listings which are fantastic for students to "data mine" and see who else they should connect with. For example, if your student is interested in the health industry and joins a related group, he or she can simply view the members and find people within their communities or who share their interests and connect with them.

- <u>Jobs listings which are fantastic as the jobs will be relevant to the group and your student's interests.</u>

- Search tools to find members and to be able to send them notes – even though you are not connected to them.

- Member statistics that offer information about members via title, location etc.

Here's an example of how I use this.

As a member of a group, I can send messages directly to fellow group members, even though I am not "connected to them." I'm currently working on an annual project where we hold a 12-hour online career webinar that features 24 of the nation's top career authors and experts. I'd like to connect with people at Sallie Mae and Facebook because both have benefited from providing their services to college students.

I'm hoping to get them involved in marketing the event.

To me, LinkedIn is a professional phone book. All I have to do is search the company name and then look at the titles produced from my search until I find the title of the person I want to connect with. When I find the right person, I look to see if we are in the same group. If we are, I go to the group page and I send that person a message.

It's an incredible way to be able to reach into a corporate structure to find the people you need to do business with.

Besides using groups to find other people to connect with, your student should be participating in group discussions. He or she can simply "like" someone's discussion or join discussions and make statements. Not only does this get your student's picture in front of others, but it gives him or her a chance to interact with professionals and build a reputation.

d) Follow companies they are interested in

Hopefully your student has a general idea about what industry he or she would like to work in. The next step for your student is to find a list of companies in that space. If he or she is interested in working in the advertising industry, he or she will quickly see a list of companies and can drill down to get additional information.

After your student builds a list, the next step is to get some background information on these companies. There are two ways companies can be researched. I like doing a search on Wikipedia. Many companies will give their history, background, and mission right there. Students can also search on LinkedIn. Companies not only have the ability to create their own company pages but within their company page, followers have access to a list of employees and management.

So why is this important?

You've heard for years that 80 percent of the people that get jobs have an inside connection, right?

When I heard that only 12 percent of the jobs that are offered come as a result of a job board posting, yet the average job seeker will spend

40 hours a month feeding and reading job boards, I realized that it is important to work smarter, not harder, it's who you know – not what you know.

So LinkedIn gives your student the incredible opportunity to connect with inside people and develop relationships with them while they are students or even after they graduate. By following the company, your student will know when jobs are posted and can reach out to the people he or she knows within that company.

When they follow companies, students receive alerts and updates when there are new hires, positions available, and/or updates being made.

It's a sure fire way to get your student's resume on top of the pile.

e) Participate in Answers

LinkedIn *Answers* gives members an opportunity to ask questions of other members within categories of interests.

In the search box, members have the option of clicking on *Answers* which will lead to the *Answers* home page. It's best your student looks around a bit to gain a perspective about how to participate, how others have participated, and acceptable customs. This is not an area where the student would ask, "Do you know of a company interested in hiring graduates?"

What he or she should be asking are questions within a field of interest that relate to issues the industry is having today or how they are relating to millennials.

Here are some examples-- for students interested in:

- HR – "How is your organization using social media to attract prospective millennials?"

- Sales – "What skills and knowledge do you recommend new graduates have when they start their first sales jobs?"

- Hospitality/Travel – "How is your organization adapting to the changes in consumer buying and traveling behaviors?"

- Health – "How do you see your organization using virtual and online health strategies in the next 3 years?"

- Government – "What do you see as emerging best practices in using the internet to better serve customers and reduce the costs of doing business?"

- Retail – "How do you see customer service in the retail industry using social media during the next 3 years to better serve customers and increase revenue?"

Get the idea?

The reason students need to participate in *Answers* is that it gives them exposure to decision makers and working professionals. It's a fantastic way for people to discuss academically (and sometimes argue) ideas and concepts. Your student's participation in *Answers* will show up in the daily news activity and everyone that is connected to will see a student's name repeated and catch an overview of his or her engagement. Savvy employers will know how to dig into this information to gain a better idea of the knowledge, work ethic, creativity and engagement of prospective employees.

I don't need to remind you that we are in a job market where 6 people are chasing every job and, depending on the job, there are dozens if not hundreds more. So if your student really wants to stand out, he or she must leave little footprints in this digital world that support how he or she is different.

I would advise your student to bring up participation on *Answers* during interviews.

When they are asked in an interview, "Do you have any questions for me?" your student could quickly bring up one or two of the questions they posed on LinkedIn *Answers* related to the industry. For example,

> "Yes, I do. I recently posed a question on LinkedIn *Answers* about how organizations were using social media to attract prospective millennials. There seemed to be a wide range of opinions on the effectiveness and benefits of it and I was curious how your organization is planning to use social media to attract prospective millennials?"

Do you see how this can set your student apart from others?

LinkedIn and social media are destined to be the dominant methods that companies and organizations will use to attract and retain employees in the future. If the company is not planning on moving in this direction, your student may not want to work there. If they are, it gives the hiring manager the ability to share the company's plans and for the two to dialogue more about it. It also gives your student the ability to ask, "How's that going for you?" and that question will lead to a discussion of issues, problems, and setbacks and give your student an opportunity to offer alternative ideas and solutions.

If your student can lead the discussion in this manner, he or she can practically write his or her own job description!

f) Share industry news and information

We talked about the importance of your student being seen in discussions and in the daily news sections of LinkedIn by participating in groups and *Answers*. There is another way for your student to show industry knowledge and business acumen by sharing updates and news that he or she is reading in trade journals, blogs and newspapers.

In this area of LinkedIn, there is a continual stream of updates from members connecting with other members, members sharing information, and members changing bio information or photos. It similar to the Facebook news feed and again the value is that it puts your student's photo and participation out there for people who have connected to him or her.

I see this area as a daily newsletter too, as I find excellent articles and discussions recommended by others that I might be interested in. So participation on LinkedIn should be relatively easy as your student already knows how to update his or her Facebook status. It's the same here.

Let's say he or she finds a great blog article and wants to share. All your student has to do is copy the URL of the article and make a statement about why he or she thinks it's a valuable read. Their statement has to be catchy to get the attention of others to get noticed. When he or she hits enter, the URL and the comment is instantly viewed by the network.

The network can "like", "recommend," and "comment" on their shared information and the status updates will show on members' profile pages to give viewers of the profile page a good overview of the kind of knowledge they share. Again, this gives prospective employers a very good overview of how savvy your student is and could be the one reason he or she makes it to the final rounds of interviews!

g) Get recommendations

Your student needs to immediately start collecting recommendations from people beginning his or her freshman year of college. Your student needs to be thinking about this for every job he or she has, because as jobs come and go, recommendations are organized per company he or she has worked for. It looks pretty darn good to see recommendations from each company where your student has been employed.

The best recommendations come from people your student has directly worked for and possibly vendors with whom he or she was involved. Recommendations from peers are OK, but will not carry as much weight.

If your student has not had work experience but has been involved in clubs and organizations, it makes perfect sense for him or her to get recommendations from the leaders and members of the club.

h) Search for jobs

One of LinkedIn's revenue sources is giving companies low cost job listings. For about $175, a firm can list a position. When you click on the *Jobs* link, it shows jobs that are compatible to your profile. You can also search for additional job openings. While having access to jobs posted in LinkedIn is great, LinkedIn has a unique feature that is not available on other job websites. LinkedIn tells you how many people in your network or group work at the company. Those people can help you get the job that you are interested in.

3) Facebook

When you graduated from college, I'm sure you were like me, you stayed in touch with a couple of classmates, but you completely lost track of the hundreds of others you interacted with. Reunions might have given you an opportunity to catch up and network, but chances are it was purely social and the meetings were limited.

<u>Unfortunately, colleges spend little to no time teaching college students how to network with each other and effectively leverage the relationships</u>. When I graduated from Kent State University, there were 2,000 others heading off into the business world and I had no clue that the person sitting next to me might be a valuable business associate, one that would help me get a job or introduce me to an alum that I might start a business with. Graduates from Harvard and Ivy League colleges instinctively know how to utilize their alumni networks.

Your student's college (more than likely) does not. So one of the first things we need to do is make sure your student knows is how to network.

You might be surprised that we are recommending your student use Facebook to look for jobs, but it has the potential to be one of the most powerful job search tools for them now and in the future.

Why?

Facebook, at the time of me writing this, is moving toward *1 billion* members. Consider some of these additional statistics and information:

- The average user is now 38 years old.

- Fifty percent of these members check their Facebook profile page every day.

- 48% of 18-34 year olds check Facebook when they wake up.

- Over 700 billion minutes a month are spent on Facebook.

- Over 200 million people access Facebook via their mobile phones.

- 48% of young people said they now get their news from Facebook.

In short, it's a happening place, the place to be, be seen, and stay in touch.

The average person spends nearly an hour a day on Facebook and I'm betting your student spends that or more time on Facebook via their computers, smart phones and smart pads.

In fact, we anticipate in the next couple years, if not next year, Facebook will be taking on LinkedIn by implementing greater controls so users can continue to create their personal lifetime scrapbook, <u>and will give them the ability to share their professional side too.</u>

Five tips to help students use Facebook professionally

Since 2005, over 90 percent of all college students have used Facebook and continue to use it.

During college, your student will have immediate access to classmates at anytime via his or her Facebook connections and that connection continues through their news feeds and updates they share every day. It's not unusual for graduating college students to have anywhere from 500 to 1500 "friends" which gives them a huge field of people to be able to reach out to when they are looking for jobs or new jobs are about to be posted in their companies.

But they will need to know

- How to control what they share and who they share it with

- How to use Facebook Events

- How to use Industry News and Updates

- About Company/Organization Fan Pages

- About applications like BranchOut and BeKnown

a) Control what they share and who they share it with

One of the first things students need to do is adopt the new Facebook Timeline option and begin to clean up who they want to have access to what. They have the ability to literally control every single post, photo, video, or bit of information they are sharing.

The Society for Human Resource Management in a recent survey found that 56% of employers are tapping into online communities like Facebook and others to search for candidates. What they may find could hurt your student's chance at getting a job.

Facebook has given your student the ability to create his or her own groups/lists of which any of their content can be limited to or shared with. For example, your student can create a group called alumni and put all their college friends in the group. He or she can create a mentor group, prospective employers group, etc. As he or she posts information he or she can elect to share the information with those individual groups.

We talked about using the daily news section of LinkedIn for your student to share news and information to build a personal brand, which can also be done on Facebook.

As they add professional relationships, they can share the same information they are sharing on LinkedIn with the smaller groups they are forming on Facebook. For example, they could share the *Answer* they posted on LinkedIn relating to the HR industry's adoption of social media for hiring on Facebook, linking to the *Answer* which will share it with the targeted contacts he or she has on Facebook. It's a nice way of getting double exposure in two different marketing channels.

Facebook gives your student the ability to double check what others will see once the lists are defined. It's worth checking. All your student has to do is click on the *View As* option and he or she will see the information that would be seen by the alumni group, business networking, hiring professionals etc. If he or she sees some holes in the content management strategy, corrections can be made and your student can be assured that only his or her alumni buddies will see the pictures from 3 years ago where everyone was drinking out of those high heeled shoes of one of the sorority members!

b) Facebook Events

By following companies and organizations fan pages, your student will be alerted about events and activities those groups are holding. Your student has the option of using Facebook's event registration system where he or she can register as "attending," "maybe," or "not attending." By participating in these events and indicating he or she is attending, his or her photo appears and the network is alerted that they plan to attend. This keeps your student's smiling face in front of people.

As we mentioned before, companies are now looking at the social media data trails prospective employees leave. If your student is showing an interest in participating in industry related webinars and events, it provides further evidence of his or her commitment to learning – a soft skill trait that nearly every company has indicated as important in its hiring decisions.

c) Industry News and Updates/ Subscribe

As your student begins to follow more companies, his or her news feed will fill up with announcements and information about and from those companies. It's a convenient way to gather news and learn about new companies.

d) Facebook Company/Organization Fan Pages

Think of Facebook as a modern day cable, TV, magazine or radio station. It's simply a new channel for people to get access to their news, information and entertainment –plus, it's replacing the telephone and email because it is also a communication channel.

Companies and organizations are clamoring to get access to this marketing channel not only because it's so VAST, but also because it's free! Think about it. Any company, organization or government agency can create a fan page that provides them the ability to:

- Share video about their products and services

- Link to drive fans to special offers and product information

- Poll to find opinions on new products and services

- Offer event registration tools to invite people to online or offline events

- Advertise products and services

- Create unique applications to engage their customer bases

- Customize their fan pages to include multiple tabs using stunning graphics, embedded video and links to resources

- And, at the same time, they plug into the nearly billion member network – all for zilch. That's a pretty good deal. In the old days you had to be in the phone book to be found. Today an organization needs to have a fan page to be found and be relevant to its customers.

For example, Pringles Potato Chips has nearly 17,000,000 people who follow it on their Facebook fan pages. That means at any time, Pringles can post a coupon offer or provide information to their 17,000,000 person network. That's not all. When the information shows up on all 17,000,000 fans news feeds, their friends will be exposed to it, too. If their friends wanted to, they could LIKE, Comment and/or share the information with their friends which can cause viral results.

In my opinion, the fan page should be for most organizations the equivalent of a newsletter. People fan an organization page because they want to learn more about it and to interact with it. It's not unusual for companies to share:

- Events

- Product information

- New job postings and new hires

- Recognition of employees

- Highlights about customers

- Industry news

- Requests for feedback via comments, or polls

When he or she fans a page, your student will receive updates on his or her news feed which he or she can quickly respond to.

Let's assume the company posts a new job opportunity. If your student has developed some in-house contacts and the job is relevant to his or career goals, your student could contact his or her in-house LinkedIn contacts and ask if they might personally put your student's resume on the desk of the person hiring for the position. Do you see how important it will be to develop this behavior over time? It's really nothing that you can turn a switch on, but when done effectively, just a little bit of effort over time can result in students getting jobs faster, with less effort.

Millions of organizations are actively using Facebook as a business marketing, communication and brand building tool. As human resources departments catch up, we anticipate your student will see more businesses using Facebook for hiring. Your student needs to perfect this behavior and make it part of his or her daily routine.

e) Facebook Applications

Facebook has made a number of brilliant moves to build a user base, increase the number of people using it and lock users to its platform. One of those is to let any organization create applications to connect with, communicate with, gather data from and engage its users. The cost? Zilch. Organizations have to create their own applications, but once they do, there is no additional cost.

That gives an organization access to information about the users which includes their email contact information. It's a fantastic opportunity. My firm, Internet Strategies Group, created a Facebook application called iBelong that enables admissions offices to connect prospective students with each other, alumni and current students. It includes games, trivia, contests and the ability to share information. Instead of sending students to the university site, all of this happens right on Facebook, where their colleges' prospective students are already!

One new application that is picking up some steam in the career area is BranchOut.

BranchOut is an application that your student will add to his or her profile page. There is no cost. By adding the application your student will agree to share some of their Facebook data with BranchOut so he or she can take advantage of services offered. Your student will also have an opportunity to share additional information if they want to fully exploit the capabilities of the service.

BranchOut describes their product as follows:

> BranchOut users leverage their Facebook friend network to find jobs, source sales leads, recruit talent, and foster relationships with professional contacts. BranchOut also operates the largest job board on Facebook with over 3 million jobs and over 20,000 internships.

It's easy to add Branchout to your profile page and once your student adds this application, he or she will be continually notified of opportunities and new connections. It is one of the premier applications on Facebook that turns Facebook into a platform much like LinkedIn. For example, your student will be able to search for a company and immediately see which of his or her friends work there or --if they don't have any friends who work there-- they will be presented with people they could connect with who are working there so they could begin to form relationships with those individuals.

Monster has created a very flexible application called BeKnown that is similar and connects job seekers with others who are working at companies that are currently hiring.

4 – Twitter

Twitter is rapidly being adopted by hiring managers as a fast and easy way to get the message out about their positions through the network of current employees, recruiters and those following the company.

Why?

Because it has over 140 million active users, half of which sign on and use Twitter daily and who produce over 230 million tweets per day, and, because it's free, too!

A simple Tweet to 1,000 followers could be picked up by 10 followers who share it with their 10 followers who, from among that group another 10 share it, and pretty soon the company is getting exposure about its position around the globe. Think about that network reach – 1,000 x 10 = 10,000 and if all 10,000 share it, a tweet would reach 100,000 people. It's incredibly fast and enables a company to "field test" a position to see if they get quality candidates before they invest in posting on a job board.

Your student will need to learn how to use Twitter as a job search tool. This will be one of those unique areas where the savvy will get in on jobs before the general public is even aware. When your student does this, he or she can also use our suggestions of building relationships via LinkedIn with alumni in that company to get the inside scoop and to have his or her resume personally delivered by the alumni to the department that is hiring and bypassing HR!

Susan Britton Whitcomb, a presenter in our Grad Career Webinar Series and author of "Tweet Your Way to a Job", suggests a job seeker start by looking at TweetMyJobs.com, a site that has over 1.5 million job tweets each month. On this site your student can drill into 10,000 subcategories to find jobs by geography, industry, position type and more.

Susan likes to say Twitter is a "barrier buster" because it gives anyone an opportunity to reach people who are at higher levels of authority. It will give users the ability to get beyond gatekeepers and go right to the people responsible for hiring positions.

Susan suggests that your student first concentrate on the companies students are looking for, then identify people within the company that your students can follow and who can direct them to the positions being hired.

She also recommends that they follow:

- Recruiters

- Job leads & feeds

- Geographic lists

- Professional development conferences

- Networking contacts and industry leaders

- Career experts with job search tips

- Internal networking contacts, competitors, clients, customers, and vendors

- Lists

Your student should build lists of target companies and individuals that are related to their careers and follow those on it. The benefit of doing this is that one can see specific tweet streams ONLY from those related to the job search. Anyone with a Twitter account is probably aware that when he or she is following an assortment of unrelated people, their stream of tweets can become overwhelming. This can cause your student to overlook the important tweets related to his or her job search. The list functionality will isolate the job tweets and will enable students to quickly review them on a daily basis.

Additional sites she recommends you look at include:

- Listoroius.com

- Twitjobsearch.com

It takes a change in your behavior to adopt the Twitter strategy as it's more than just a tool to search for job opportunities that are being posted by organizations, but it also a way to show knowledge and thought leadership.

Once your student follows a person at company they can show their interest in the company and/or appreciation of the content they share by:

- Shoutouts

- Retweets

Shoutouts are a simple way of repeating the person's/company's name and sharing a tweet with a personal network. Retweets take seconds and simply allow one to click on "retweet" to repeat someone else's tweet.

Most people and organizations have tools to track who is talking about them so the more your student's name shows up in their tracking tools, the greater chance they will have in developing a relationship with the company insiders and eventually get an inside track on jobs and openings.

SUMMARY

This is one of the most important chapters for you to concentrate on as it represents new techniques and strategies that did not exist-- in some cases-- even 6 months ago, and yet, **all are becoming dominate recruiting and job search strategies.**

While you may not be anticipating that you will find yourself unemployed anytime soon, these are strategies YOU should be adopting for yourself. Get in and experience this process and you'll be able to get your student up to speed too!

COMING UP

Now we are going to get into some of our recommended ways to help your son or daughter get a job. You are about to pick up our top 7 ways you can be a resource to your child and give him or her some areas on which to concentrate that career professionals have proven to work. They don't have to do every single one, let them choose just one area and work it.

The three hardest things in the world are steel, diamonds, and to understand yourself.

- Ben Franklin, Statesman

YOUR TO DO'S AND NOTES!

_____

_____

_____

_____

_____

_____

_____

_____

_____

_____

CHAPTER RESOURCES

Visit Your College Career Center!

LinkedIn Primer for Grads

www.theunemployedgrad.com

We'll show you how your grad should be using Linkedin to network with alumni and build relationships starting their freshman year! Free!

7 BUILDING BLOCKS OF YOUR STUDENT'S CAREER PLAN AND JOB SEARCH STRATEGY.

Your student needs a blue print, a plan he or she can follow throughout the dozen+ job searches during a lifetime. Your student will be more confident and stay focused on where he or she wants to go!

You've heard the phrase, "If you don't know where you are going – you are already there!"

Your student's career could be like that. Without a plan-- no better yet-- without a written plan, your student will not have a blue print that will guide his or her job search process and career.

We believe that in order to really know what your student wants to do, and know where he or she is going, your student needs to take a look inside, and really get to know what it is that turns him or her on and what he or she is really interested in.

Your student will need to:

- Identify who he or she is by completing assessment tests in - behaviors, skills, personality, etc.

- Identify what industries he or she wants to work in.

- Create a list of target companies and people to contact.

- Identify what types of positions and responsibilities interest him or her.

Next your student will need to:

- Build & clean up online profiles and websites - LinkedIn, Facebook, Twitter.

- Participate in campus clubs and activities to show leadership

- Develop his or her personal branding and thought leadership components.

With this foundation your student needs to continue to identify activities and strategies that will help get him or her where he or she wants to go.

SEVEN BUILDING BLOCKS

To help you take your student through this process, we've identified seven building blocks or components of career and job search strategies that will be critical in helping him or her enjoy a happy, successful career!

1. Encourage your student to use the career center and explore career options.

2. Have your student explore jobs that match their interests.

3. Have your student create a **personal career profile.**

4. Have your student create a written <u>job search strategy</u>.

5. Have your student create a written **career plan.**

6. Make sure your student has the fundamental job search skills.

7. Encourage your student to build a professional network.

This chapter has an enormous amount of suggestions, ideas and tips in it so plan on taking some quality time with it so you can design strategies with your student that will provide the greatest degree of success for the least amount of effort.

1) Encourage your student **to visit the career center.**

If your student is in college and/or just about to enter college, this is our number one suggestion.

We shared data previously that indicated that over 60% of college seniors either never go to the career center or visit less than twice.

Why?

The career center is essentially another campus club. As a result, your student will NEVER be required to step foot in their door.

In our opinion, the career center should be the first stop on the campus tour. It's probably not as impressive as the library, student recreation center, or even the student union but for parents and students of this generation, the information the career center provides can help students get jobs faster and get jobs related to their careers. However, few tours include it.

The survey we mentioned earlier and that UCLA has been conducting for the past 40 years showed that 78.9 percent of incoming students expect their college education will give them a better shot at a more successful career, and is proof that <u>the career center should have an elevated position on campuses.</u> Smart colleges will take this fact and after ramping up resources and services in the career center will use it as a way to differentiate their college from others.

Why don't colleges focus on their career centers as part of their campus tours?

Possibly because there hasn't been a demand in the past, or more likely because the average career center is a relatively modest office that is tucked away in a converted boiler room or off the beaten path. No joke, here is a quote I picked up from a newspaper article:

> "There aren't many walk-ins at either of Career Services' two current locations, which happen to be on opposite sides of campus. One student referred to our current location as a 'dungeon' because it is in a dreary basement, said the director of Career Services."

Regardless, I think it's important that the college shows the importance of career development and begin to take the opportunity to show students and parents how important this department is and even to hand to them a recommendation about how they should use these services during the four years on campus (and over the summer)!

However, the career center will be an important part of your student's career development strategy. Your student can get a good start in developing a plan by using the services the career center provides.

I realize that in chapter two we suggested the career center does not have the resources and staff to help all students. However, I've never known any to turn students away. So your student would be wise to take advantage of this department's expertise and services.

The career center will:

- Have assessments your student can take to verify and quantify his or her interests, passions and skills.

- Information about industries, companies and job title/responsibilities.

- Provide practice interviewing sessions.

- Provide access to information on how to develop job search skills.

- Connect your student with interview opportunities on campus.

- Give guidance about how to create a great resume.

…and much more.

I highly suggest that as part of your student's career exploration strategy that he or she plans on a monthly visit to the career center.

- During his or her **freshman** year, your student should avail himself or herself of every assessment and test the college offers and request the career staff to explain and interpret the results. Career exploration as well as assessments should be the focus.

- By his or her **sophomore** year, your student should be meeting with career center professionals monthly and talking about the industries that best suit the results they received from their assessments and tests and to gain advice and direction about what companies they could be approaching for internships. It doesn't hurt to start attending job fairs as some companies will be looking for interns too!

- By his or her **junior year**, your student should be working on his or her resume and gaining additional advice and guidance about how to use social media in a job search.

- In his or her **senior year**, your student should be not only be attending events, campus visits by recruiters, and having staff help him or her with practice interviews, but he or she should also be asking for leads on companies that traditionally hire students.

Remind your student that by spending more time developing his or her job search strategy, he or she will have a better chance of having a job by graduation day-- which means they will go from eating pizza to being able to afford steak, while their friends are eating peanut butter and jelly sandwiches and living at home worrying about having to pay back their student loans.

Let's look at it another way.

If your student has a job lined up by graduation day that pays $3,000 per month, and it takes the average grad 8 months to get a job, he or she will end up $24,000 better off. If your student visited the career center 8 times a year or 32 times by the time he or she graduated, each visit would have earned your student $750.

Not bad for an hour's visit!

2) Explore jobs that match their interests

One of the most important steps in developing a career plan is narrowing down what your student wants to do and the cost of not taking this step is great!

- Changing majors while in college can result in having to go a 5th and sometimes a 6th year of college

- Studies indicate that over 60% of us do not work in the careers we prepared for while in college.

- Less than 50% of students that start college will finish.

The Department of Labor Statistics indicates that 17 million people are working in jobs that do not require a college degree!

If this is one of the most important decisions we ever make, why do we spend so little time on it? I think it comes back to not knowing what steps to take to find out what kind of career, industry, company and job is really a good fit.

Here are some of the elements your student should be doing and thinking about as they go through the process of choosing a career:

a) Take career assessments

b) Job shadow & complete internships

c) Research industries and companies

a) Assessments

What process did you use to choose your career?

For decades some pretty smart people and organizations have been developing a battery of tests that are designed to give us a more scientific, predictable way of narrowing down career choices so we can identify which careers are a natural fit for us.

Yet they are grossly underutilized.

- Does your student know what he or she wants to do?

- Has your student taken a battery of assessments?

Chances are your student had a better idea of what he or she wanted to be when at the age of 5, than he or she does as a teenager heading off to college.

It's surprising to me that every student isn't given a battery of assessments that include:

- Behavior/Personality

- Skills

- Interests

- Branding

..tests, if NOT the summer prior to entering college, at least during his or her first year of college.

A student and parent armed with this information, and the advice of a professional interpreter of the information, can do more to set a student on a successful career path then you can imagine. <u>I can't stress the importance of gaining feedback from someone that knows how to interpret the tests.</u> A professional can help your student read between the lines and help him or her get a better understanding of what he or she would be happiest and most successful at.

If the career center doesn't offer these services, there are career coaches that can step in and help your student. It's not that expensive. It might require us to cut back on our visits to Starbucks, but it will be worth it.

Indulge me to share some details on each of these assessments.

BEHAVIOR PROFILE

Behavior profiles will help your student understand the type of person he or she is and how he or she needs to communicate with others. We particularly like Tony Alessandra's Platinum Rule behavior test. Tony's online profile will help your student determine if they are a:

1. Director

2. Socializer

3. Relater

4. Thinker

Based on the results, students can learn about other behavior styles and how they should communicate with other people based on them. For an example, if your student is a socializer, he or she will quickly learn that he or she can't relate and/or communicate with a thinker as well as someone more like himself or herself.

By taking Tony's test your student will learn tricks and proven strategies that will help him or her to communicate and relate with others. This will be important for your student in building personal friendships on their dorm floor, with faculty, and future bosses.

Your student should also gain a better understanding of his or her personality as it will offer another indicator to the best career path, industries and positions he or she would not only excel at, but also those your student should avoid.

In a business environment it will be critical for your student to learn behavior and communication styles if he or she is going to work on projects, sell ideas or products, or handle customers.

SKILLS

Skills assessments help companies measure a candidate's skill level. They provide an employer and your student a better understanding of whether he or she will qualify for specific tasks, and/or responsibilities.

Skill tests will show a candidate's level of proficiency by identifying if he or she has basic, intermediate or advanced skills.

These are critical assessments because it gives your student a true picture of how good he or she is at a task. At the same time, skill assessments can identify what he or she needs to work on to improve skills if the job or career path he or she has chosen requires more advanced skills then your student currently has. It's better to know these things now then to have to pick those skills up later. Many skills test will also show your student in what percentile they rank for certain traits.

INTERESTS

Interest assessments will help your student learn about his or her preferences. Interest assessments suggest that people can be loosely classified into six categories:

1. Realistic

2. Investigative

3. Artistic

4. Social

5. Enterprising

6. Conventional

This type of assessment should probably be done before your student goes to college so they have some general understanding of interests and how those might relate to careers and ultimately a major.

The benefit of taking interest assessments early is that college majors and careers can also be sorted into these same categories. After taking the assessments, your student can look at college majors and careers that may be consistent with your preferences. Your student will be more likely to be satisfied with career choices that are consistent with his or her skills, interests and values.

BRANDING

Companies are known to have brands. Coke, Pepsi and just about any company you can think of worries constantly about their brand images. They conduct surveys to find out what personality types like their products, what political interests those people have and much more. Since the late 90's, business experts have been suggesting that people are "brands," too.

William Arruda is a bestselling author and personal branding expert. William developed an online branding tool that enables students to anonymously gather feedback from friends, family, acquaintances, and teachers in order to help them determine how others see them. It's really a nifty little online survey.

After filling in some basic information and the email addresses of the people they want feedback from, the program sends a request asking the others to fill in a quick form to pick words that identify the person. The results come back to your student's own personal dashboard and provide him or her a snapshot of how other people see them.

Many times this is entirely different than what your student perceives of himself or herself.

NO WRONG ANSWERS

There are two things your student needs to keep in mind when taking assessments.

First, there is no wrong answer! They need to take assessments and provide honest responses without influences, or help from ANYONE.

Second, if we haven't made it clear enough yet, your student should spend time with the career services office, or you should consider having a professional coach that is certified in these areas to provide your student feedback, and help him or her gain a better understanding of what the assessments mean. This step alone will give your student a solid foundation from which he or she can begin to build a future.

All of us have preconceived visions of what our children could or should be doing. Some who are in the professional world envision their children following in their footsteps as attorneys, accountants, pastors, or even politicians. Your job is to make sure you have a clear picture of what your student's assessments are saying about your student and to give your student the feedback and advice so your student can determine if he or she is cut out to be what WE want them to be. If the assessments come back otherwise, and your student does not show an interest, then your job is to back off and let your student find his or her own way.

b) Job shadowing and Internships

Now that your student has some directions it will be extremely important for your student to get an idea of the day to day activities and responsibilities of someone within the fields in which he or she shows interest.

Job shadowing either involves visiting a place of work and simply observing a contact, or in today's virtual world, it could include 2-3 hours of connecting with a contact via Skype and observing phone calls, meetings, document review etc. Ideally, job shadowing should be done during the high school years so your student can begin to grasp the realities of working in a business.

My son's high school required sophomores to spend a day job shadowing someone. Ben decided he wanted to job shadow a professional skateboarder, Rob Dyrdek who at the time lived in San Diego. I told him as long as he stayed with his Uncle Jack, a world class marathon swimmer, I'd use my airline points to fly him out there. For two days, Ben skateboarded with Rob and his cousin all around San Diego and Los Angeles. Ben had a chance to see a radically different way to earn a living.

Now, nearly 7 years, later Rob has two TV shows on MTV, has his own clothing and shoe line, has opened a dozen skate board parks around the country for kids to "safely" skate in their communities and has just announced a new business partnership called IVI that will market highend sun glasses. Ben's job shadow opened his eyes to how one can have fun in business and make money, too. I'm confident that experience will guide his career decisions in life and may in time find Ben working within one of Rob's rapidly expanding businesses!

My daughter Annie has been accepted to Ohio State and is seriously considering nursing as a major and profession. She's an incredibly gifted, empathetic and giving person that fits the personality type necessary to provide care to patients, but I really want her to get into a hospital environment and/or office environment to get a feel for the day to day responsibilities nurses have if for no other reason but to help her identify a specific area of nursing she may be interested in.

Job shadowing opportunities and internships are critical for students to gain an inside look at careers and positions that interest them. While schools focus on volunteer days, it might make sense that students have at least 4 job shadowing opportunities before they graduate.

I would encourage your student to get the job description of the person whom he or she is job shadowing so they have a better idea of what that person's responsibilities are.

c) Research industries and companies

Assessments will only give your student feedback and clues that will help him or her make the right career choice, but they will also need to pick up a book and/or search online to learn more about industries and then drill into specific areas like:

- Health
- Entertainment
- Media
- Retail
- Recreation
- Education

..etc.

Next your student will need to begin to evaluate the specific positions and responsibilities that he or she is going to thrive in. This is a process that nearly everyone overlooks.

Other factors students should consider as they are choosing their careers would be the type of companies or organizations they want to work in. Will they find the greatest satisfaction and/or success working in:

- Medium and large corporations?
- Small business?
- Government agencies and/or state local government?
- Volunteer organizations?
- Nonprofits?

Or, should your student start his or her own business?

The Millennial generation (born 1978-2000), while large in numbers, is significantly smaller than the 79 million Boomer generation born between 1945 and 1964.

A recent report I read indicated that 40% of the 21 million federal, state, and local government positions will need to be filled in the next decade as Boomers who have worked all their lives to reach management positions begin to retire. In fact, beginning January 1st, 2011 and every single day for the next 19 years, more than 10,000 Baby Boomers will reach the age of 65. I have to believe there will be some really great jobs that will open up as more experienced people step in to fill those positions.

A study by the Partnership for Public Service, that surveyed 35,000 college students revealed that only 2.3 percent of those polled plan to work for the federal government and that 6 percent say they want to work in any government job, be it local, state or federal level.

Depending on your student's interests and goals, there appears to be a steady turn over in this employment sector.

DOES YOUR STUDENT THINK LIKE A MILLENNIAL?

Researchers are finding your student's generation has different characteristics and aspirations than other generations. Like other generations, they have watched their parents' and grandparents' generations and lifestyles and they have identified areas in which they are forging their own ways.

Here's how a study by Yale economic professor Lisa Kahn identifies Millennials:

1. They are more risk adverse.

2. Won't invest as much into the stock market or any one job.

3. They question traditional hierarchies.

4. They believe luck plays a role in success.

5. More are willing to settle.

6. They are less likely to put themselves back in the job market.

7. They're more sheltered and want to stay that way.

8. They want answers immediately.

9. They are more socially awkward.

10. They don't want to report to anyone!

11. They are more modest and realistic.

12. They work well in teams and hate conflict.

13. They value hard work.

14. More are launching startups.

Does any of this sound like your student? Some of these traits could result in employment and advancement issues.

For example:

- A student that questions traditional hierarchies is going to get frustrated if he or she picks a company that is conservative, stuck in its ways, and has a strong pecking order. This student probably won't do well at IBM!

- If your student is one that does not like conflict, he or she is not going to do well in businesses where conflict and discourse is the norm.

- If your student is unwilling to invest 100 percent of himself or herself in a position, management will notice and your student's opportunity for advancement will be stunted.

It will be important to have a discussion with your student to review these points to help him or her gain a better idea of what kind of industry, company or culture will best fit with who he or she is.

CHOOSE WISELY AS CAREERS OPPORTUNITIES COME AND GO

Since the early 1900's, industrialization has eliminated farming and similar jobs. Then, manufacturing jobs were displaced by robots that worked for pennies per hour. By 2000, we saw the internet starting to eliminate jobs and industries. When it comes to careers, your student will have to be flexible, because the career they choose today may be all but eliminated within 5 years.

Well, folks, there are more changes coming, and more than likely we are going to see even more rapid changes and reduced job opportunities as the full effect of globalization and smarter computers --all connected by the internet-- takes hold.

One simple invention or refinement like the iPad can change the book industry, computer hardware industry, and magazine and news industries, and affect areas we'd never dream would be affected. Somewhere right now a group is involved in a startup that is developing applications that could put even your job at risk.

Annie Lowrey of Slate Magazine wrote about a start-up company called "E la Carte" that is out to eliminate some 2.4 million waiter and waitress positions.

> The company "has produced a kind of souped-up iPad that lets you order and pay right at your table. The brainchild of a bunch of M.I.T. engineers, the nifty invention, known as the Presto, might be found at a restaurant near you soon.

> You select what you want to eat and add items to a cart. Depending on the restaurant's preferences, the console could show you nutritional information, ingredients lists and photographs. You can make special requests, like 'dressing on the side' or 'quintuple bacon.' When you're done, the order zings over to the kitchen, and the Presto tells you how long it will take for your items to come out.

> Bored with your companions? Play games on the machine. When you're through with your meal, you pay on the console, splitting the bill item by item if you wish and paying however you want. You can even have your receipt e-mailed to you.

> Each console goes for $100 per month. If a restaurant serves meals eight hours a day, seven days a week, it works out to 42 cents per hour per table — making the Presto cheaper than even the very cheapest waiter and less expensive for guests who now don't pay a tip.

We are moving toward a self service economy that will continue to decimate blue collar and white collar jobs.

If we've not made this clear yet, let me repeat,

> If you really want your student to stand out in this crowded market, your student will need to invest a minimum of 20-40 hours each year he or she is in college in career exploration, creating a career plan and job search strategy.

Your student can control his or her career path if he or she has a better idea of where he or she needs to be.

You don't want your student to wake up 20 years into a career, unhappy with where he or she is and feeling depressed because he or she wished he or she had followed a path based on skills, interests, and passions he or she had always had. If your college is not offering and administering results to assessments, you need to step in and make this part of the natural process your student goes through in his or her college experience.

3) Develop a personal career profile.

One of the first steps in creating a written career management strategy is to develop a personal career profile.

A personal career profile is an outline of what your student will be looking for in a career. It helps him or her put down on paper strengths, interests and passions which will help guide your student to choose a career and job that fits his or her profile.

It's simple to do and it's designed to eliminate options and career choices rather than to define exactly what your student wants.

There are about 50 different questions your student could answer to build a personal career profile, but for the sake of brevity and to keep this book a reasonable length, here are 15:

- Indicate the size of the company you want to work for.

- Do you want to work for a family business, nonprofit corporation, association, or an educational or government organization?

- Do you eventually want a leadership position?

- Are you looking for a firm that provides quick promotions?

- What kind of company culture are you interested in, laid back or professional?

- Are you willing to work more than 40 hours a week if needed?

- Do you want a position where you work out of the office more than in the office?

- Do you want to travel?

- Are you looking for a position where you have set duties or duties that vary from day to day?

- What type of clients do you want to interact with? (Retail, Corporate, Community)

- Does it matter what the average age of the company employees are?

- Are you interested in working within a big city, small city, or suburb?

- What characteristics are you looking for in a boss and/or leadership in the company?

- How do you want to be managed by your boss?

- Do you prefer to work for younger, older, men or women?

Got the idea?

Once completed, this should become the foundation on which your student chooses some job opportunities and eliminates others. Your student should consider this a living document. It should be updated every 3 years.

Once your student has completed this, your student is in a better position to begin to do online research to look for companies and positions within those companies that might interest him or her. The career center or library is a good resource to find government lists and others that will enable your student to drill into companies.

30 SECOND ELEVATOR PITCH

We mentioned earlier that your student only has a few minutes to prove his or her worth in interviews. It doesn't matter if it's on the phone or in person, your student has to come across as confident, knowledgeable and the type of person the hiring manager is looking for.

With so many people looking for jobs, hiring managers are not looking at your student the way that you do. Their number one goal is to find just one reason why they should NOT bring the person back or pass on them for a second interview. That may sound strange but it's true. Hiring managers are looking at up to 250 or more resumes for any one position and narrowing them down to another group for phone interviews and narrowing that group down to a very small group, say 3, that they will bring in for a personal interview.

Unfortunately most students don't do any preparation for their interviews. Like social situations in college, students rely on their personal charm and think that smiles will get them by. It just doesn't work when that's everyone's strategy. If that were the case, only the best looking people with the best smiles would move to the next interview.

Your student is going to need to develop his or her 30 second elevator speech to help him or her stand out. Salespeople, entrepreneurs -- literally everyone-- needs a 30 second elevator speech to share with others that will help them stand out. Your student's 30 second elevator speech has to not only show what he or she has done to develop unique, relevant skills, but how those skills will help the company he or she is interviewing with.

Here are a few tips on how your student can develop an elevator speech:

1. Write down the top five work or personal experiences. These experiences should show problems, how or what one did to be a part of the solution and the effects of those ideas and/or solutions.

2. Take each of the 5 above and edit them down to a paragraph.

3. Look at the personal branding feedback from family, friends, and others to include the keywords, phrases and comments they have made. They might include something like, "Others see me as a go to person for advice--that is, as proactive and getting things done before deadlines. "

4. Now look for themes or similarities and techniques used to solve them.

5. Take the top two themes as well as the situations and examples and begin to summarize them into a 30 second elevator pitch. The pitch doesn't have to be 30 seconds; it's more a term than a requirement. Generally your student should aim for about a 350 word pitch that will take on average about 2 ½ minutes to say.

6. Next after writing down the pitch, say it until it's committed to memory and so that it sounds authentic and natural

7. Now share it with others and encourage them to ask questions. These people may ask for details, examples, or clarification. Write down their questions and prepare additional statements that support their questions

So now it's a matter of practice, practice, practice. The more your student practices and drills this process, the more comfortable your student will be when he or she goes on his or her first interview.

4) Encourage your student to create a written job search strategy.

Our research has shown that only 5% of college grads have written job search strategies. That means 95% of college grads today, simply "wing it" when it comes to looking for a job and interviewing.

Three of the most important fundamentals of looking for a job include:

a) Developing a job search strategy

b) Working the plan

c) Setting and reaching daily goals

When we surveyed the Class of 2011 and asked how much time they spent on their job search, 60 percent indicated they spent between 1-5 hours per week. That just about floored us and confirmed something Richard Bolles, author of *What's the Color of Your Parachute?* said in a previous webinar.

One of the reasons we think graduates spend so little time on their job search is that they just don't know how to look for a job and when they finish with the few things they know how to do, they stop. This not only guarantees it will take them longer to get a job, but they probably will miss techniques that would have given them unbelievable new opportunities!

WHAT IS A WRITTEN JOB SEARCH STRATEGY?

A job search strategy is a simple document that your student creates that will provide a framework in which he or she can conduct a job search. Think of it as a job description for the new job as a "Job Seeker".

It's a process, a plan, a step by step guide, that will help your student maximize time, keep focused, and help get a job faster, with less effort. It's designed to keep your student moving forward even when it appears nothing is working. A written job search strategy will help your student keep focused on the tactics and steps required to get a job.

If you've been in a job search, you know it's easy to get disoriented, disappointed, and dejected. Every time you get these feelings, it puts a giant road block in front of you. Your enthusiasm and commitment is replaced with an overwhelming sense of futility and you risk falling into a period of inactivity and an emotional low.

The job search process is a numbers game.

Author, Tony Beshara likes to remind his job seekers that it will take 100 calls to reach 10 hiring managers of which 2 will have a job available. That coupled with the fact that it will take 16 interviews to get a job are well documented by Tony as he tracked the progress of the 8,000 people he has put into new jobs over the past 3 decades.

Developing a job search strategy takes time. That's why we suggest your student gets started as early as he or she can and continues to build on the process.

If your student doesn't have goals, chances are he or she will spin wheels. Goals help keep your student focused on what is important and provides you evidence your student is committed to the search. If your student is not reaching goals and has been putting an honest effort into the process, you can be a resource and give your student alternative ideas.

Some of the goals we might suggest your student commit to each day are:

1. Number of new people added to professional network

2. Number of resumes posted on job boards

3. Number of follow up emails and phone calls to companies interviewed with

4. Hours/minutes spent on personal career development

5. Number of new job opportunities found

6. Number of alumni/network contacted

7. Number of calls made

8. Number of companies visited

9. Number of personal contacts made

10. Research conducted

The plan doesn't have to include all of these each day. We only offer them as a way to get your student started thinking about what to include. Some of these might be included in daily goals, others in weekly or even monthly goals.

Chances are – you've invested a good deal of money in your student's education, where faculty staff and others made requests from your student on a regular basis. We would have hoped the college was also requiring your student to create this type of plan, but they are not, so you've got to step into that vacuum of leadership and make demands and requirements of them.

You aren't asking the impossible from your student.

Your student is in college or has completed college. He or she has completed reports, met in group sessions, pulled all nighters and has done it only with minor grumbling. So building this strategic plan, in my mind, is just a final thesis!

You are also doing your student a huge favor by requiring your student to develop a written job search strategy. You are making your student a better prospective employee. This process will also help your student understand the difficulty of getting a job which will increase your student's desire to keep the job!

Your student has to understand that they need to commit a 40 hour week after college to finding a job. If he or she wants to take 2 months off to find himself or herself, remind your student that if he or she were earning $3,000 a month, they are making a $6,000 decision by delaying the job search.

Remind your student of the kind of vacation he or she could take with $6,000!

Frankly, in our opinion, your student's goal should be to get into the work world as fast as he or she can and build a strategy that will enable him or her to save 6 months of salary so at any time your student wants to change careers or take time off between careers, he or she can do so.

DAILY ROUTINE

One of the most important parts of the job search strategy is having a repeatable and measurable daily routine. The daily routine should drive the career and job search plan.

The nice thing about a job search process is your student can break up their day into a series of activities to prevent boredom from repetition. For example, to help your student get started on the right foot, your student should pretend he or she is already working. So what do you do when you are already working? You are probably getting up at 6:00 a.m. to shower, dress and drive to work.

So that should be your student's routine.

Up at least by 6:00 a.m. and ideally showered and in front of a computer, reviewing Google alerts that arrived overnight providing information about companies hiring, getting new contracts, and reporting new sales, etc., within industries in which your student is interested.

A schedule might look like this:

6:30 to 8:30	Review Google Alerts, Tweets, Facebook and LinkedIn for job mentions and follow ups
8:30 to 10:00	Review job boards like AfterCollege and Indeed for new job listings. Visit the college job board to check on new listings
10:00 to 10:30	Take a walk or quick break
10:30 to 12:00	Contact network to give them an update on what you are doing and get leads on companies that might be expanding
12:00 to 1:00	Have lunch with a friend, mentor or someone in a company or industry you are interested in being a part of
1:00 to 3:00	Visit companies you've been calling and drop in to share new information about yourself
3:00 to 5:00	Call businesses you found in your morning research
5:00 to 6:00	Eat
7:00 to 9:00	Read career books, take career courses and/or continue to work on career and job search strategy

The key to a job search is to set up this routine and stick with it.

Not only will it get your student more interviews and a job quicker but he or she will end up having a choice of jobs from which to choose. Your student will be in a better position to negotiate a better salary package if a number of offers are coming in at the same time. If your student doesn't adhere to this recommended strategy, he or she will radically reduce the number of opportunities and choices presented.

5) Have your student create a written career plan.

Let's take a look at what components we've added to our career plan so far. We've:

- Taken assessments and researched career opportunities

- Developed a personal career profile

- Created a job search strategy

Now we need to create a Career Plan.

The first two, in our opinions are the foundations of what your student is going to need to do to get a first job. If your student nails this process the first time, it will make the subsequent 10-14 he or she will have by the age of 38 easier.

It's a process that pays off. Spending just an hour a month doing something related to a career plan will lead to:

- Improved job satisfaction

- Better marketability and career advancement

- Increased professional development

- More control of one's destiny

In addition, your student's friends will admire the fact that your student seems to have his or her path already laid out.

So now we want your student to begin to think a bit longer range and look into the future to see what he or she wants to be doing 3, 6, 9 and 20 years from now. The reasons we want your student to go through this exercise is that your student needs to:

- Visualize where he or she wants to be

- Build the plan to get there

Without a written career plan, your student may bump from job to job potentially without building on previous knowledge and success.

So here are a few exercises your student can take to begin to create his or her career strategy.

- Determine the level of responsibilities and titles desired in 3, 5 and 10 years

- Identify the earning ranges desired in 3, 5, and 10 years

- Identify what triggers, events, issues that will cause your student to move on to the next position

Think of a career plan as a business plan. It's a plan that will outline where your student wants to take their "business"! Just like a business plan, your graduate's plan will need to have core components.

For example, we recommend that at minimum it includes:

1. Career Plan Summary

2. Career Plan Vision & Mission

3. Career Goals

4. Career Market Analysis

5. Career Path

6. Networking Strategy

7. Career Plan Conclusion

Career Plan Summary

Provide a simple introductory statement that identifies the purpose of the career plan

Career Plan Vision & Mission

Your student will identify an overall vision and mission statement that he or she can refer back to as he or she considers job opportunities in the future. The Vision and Mission is founded on the results of the assessments and the personal passions of your graduate, including what he or she wants to do in life.

Career Goals

A critical component of a career plan is goals. Your student can fill in the blanks on the information requested above but without firm time deadlines and goals, chances are these will never be achieved. Their career plan might include goals like:

- I will get my first promotion by _____

- I will be earning _____ by ___/__/__.

- I will reach the title of _____ by ___/__/__.

Career Market Analysis

Your student needs to include in his or her career plan a review of the industries he or she is going to pursue to make sure there is a market that supports his or her mission and vision. If your student is interested in becoming a pilot, but the prospects for pilots will be diminished due to "drone controlled" aircraft, your student needs to at least be aware of the risk he or she will face so that he or she can adapt when the time is right.

Career Path

A career path includes an outline of jobs your student wants to have in the next 3, 5, 10 and 20 years. This is one of the more important steps as it will help keep your student moving towards a goal. It will also remind your student at specific points in time that he or she needs to be moving out of the current position and to start looking for the next position he or she envisions.

Networking Strategy

Because networking is so very important, we'll want your student to put down on paper what he or she will do to build a network. This might include strategies to build it both electronically and through one-on-one relationships. Like other parts of the career plan, your student needs to set goals and target dates to accomplish things.

Career Plan Conclusion

The career plan conclusion is a simple summary that identifies the outcome of the strategy.

The career plan should be part of a New Year's resolution. Something your student looks at each year and to identify if he or she is on track or not. While your student is reviewing it, he or she should be evaluating:

- The job search strategy

- What he or she did the previous year to improve soft skills

- How he or she handled a network

The point is that it will be important that this becomes a learned behavior, something your student does like brushing his or her teeth.

6) Make sure your student has fundamental job search skills

Getting a job is a combination of skill, knowledge and art. There are no short cuts. When we take them, it usually ends badly!

There are 3 really important job search skills we think your student must master. If your student doesn't have a good understanding and mastery of these, there's a good chance that it will derail and impede progress, making your student less confident and causing your student to procrastinate and not stick with the plan.

The three are:

1. Networking

2. Interviewing

3. Knowing where and how to search

NETWORKING

There are thousands of books written about networking techniques that will help graduates pick up tips and techniques they need meet people. As we mentioned earlier, the Stanford Shyness Clinic has found that 60% of us consider ourselves shy.

As a result of being shy we:

- Are generally uncomfortable at events.

- Will be less likely to be the first person reaching out to meet others.

- Generally have a close circle of friends.

- Find it more difficult to network with others.

Learning to network is not simply learning to put oneself out there and shake hands with others, but it involves:

1. Building a professional network of people.

2. Targeting the right people to be part your network.

3. Providing value to your network and recognizing them for their achievements.

4. Managing your network by periodically reviewing correspondence, contacts, and feedback.

Many people think networking is a gift for the few that are extroverted, and naturally love to meet and talk to others. It certainly helps to be extroverted but, that's no guarantee as professional networking requires the due diligence and completion of the steps listed above.

These skills don't come naturally – they come from training and education.

Remember, because 80 percent of us get jobs through the networks we keep, this will be one of the most important skills your student can acquire – possibly more important than his or her degree!

I read an article by Dr. Ivan Misner that really resonated with me in 2005. , Dr. Misner is a professor and the founder of the Business Networking International Group (BNI.com), with thousands of chapters around the globe. In his article on Entreprenuer.com he said:

> "I recently surveyed over 1,400 business people and 88 percent of the respondents said they never had any college course that even covered the topic of networking! I'm not talking about an entire course on the subject (they are almost non-existent); I'm talking about ANY course that simply covered the topic in school. Yet, based on another survey of over 2,500 business people from around the world, 75 percent said they got most of their business through networking!

Don't expect your student's college to teach networking.

Networking is something your student will have to learn on his or her own, and frankly you will do your student a favor if you start him or her out today with the right skills to network rather than him or her trying to pick them up little by little over a 40 year career.

INTERVIEWING

I was on a flight to London sitting next to a young man that had just been accepted to the London School of Economics. He has decided to get more education from a prestigious college because after 13 interviews for a position in the same Wall Street firm, he ended up the second choice - with no job offer.

Now that's competition.

Your student needs to understand that getting an opportunity to interview is a like winning the Lotto. It doesn't happen to everyone. As a result, they should not go into an interview without being fully prepared! You've been telling your student for his or her entire life, and he or she has also been hearing it from teachers, coaches and advisors: *practice makes perfect.* That holds true with interviewing.

Unfortunately the average person NEVER practices for an interview. That's right NEVER.

Can you imagine that?   Remember some of the facts we've talked about:

- According to Tony Beshara, author of the *Job Search Organizer* it takes 100 calls to reach 10 hiring managers of which 2 will have a job to fill.

- The average hiring manager is getting as many as 250 applications per job and keyword algorithms scientifically throw out 90 percent of them, giving 25 for the hiring manager to narrow down to 3.

- It will take the average job seeker 16 interviews to get a job.

The incredible gauntlet one has to go through to get an interview warrants practicing EVERY time.

As hard as it is to get to an interview, few people put any investment in time to practice. Remember the people with whom your student is interviewing are sharp, analytical, and professionally trained people that can within seconds pick up hesitations; identify shortcomings, insecurities and/or personality issues that might not fit within the culture of the company.

My oldest daughter has been working as an actress in Los Angeles since she was 15 years old. Now 27, she still prepares for each audition she goes on. Her manager emails her a script, she spends an hour practicing, finds a wardrobe that fits the part, and depending on whether it's a guest starring role in a feature film or hot TV series, she may even pay an acting coach to practice with her and to gain his/her advice. Then she heads to the audition. In LA, you can invest 90 minutes to drive 15 miles.   I've always admired her passion and tenacity in going through the audition process. She can have as many as 3-4 auditions in a week that she has to prepare for. April knows that she has to be perfect in every way, so she practices, practices and practices.

Using April as a benchmark, I find it inconceivable that someone does not prepare for their interviews. They are going to be up against other very incredible candidates, some that will have the savvy business and interviewing skills that can overcome shortcomings in their resume and experience.

Here are seven things your student needs to do to prepare for interviews:

1. Research the company. Read their press releases, Google their name to find issues, competitive situations, and industry news.

2. Look up the person they are interviewing with on LinkedIn to find common points or information they can slip into the conversation.

3. Find alumni and/or people your student is connected to that work within the company and call to have a short conversation about things your student can bring up to share his or her understanding and knowledge of the company.

4. Review the company mission, vision and goals.

5. Visit the company's LinkedIn page and sort through the people that work there to learn more about what they do.

6. Finally, do a practice interview. I don't care if it's you, a friend or a coach, but your student needs to spend at least an hour going through a series of questions, so he or she can practice dropping in the knowledge they picked up in their research.

Ah, and one final point. Your student needs to have written down a series of questions he or she can refer back to during the interview. When the prospective employer asks, "Do you have any questions for me?" He or she needs to be prepared.

Not everyone will agree with this, but something I picked up from my father years ago was a reminder to friend the assistants of decision makers. It might not be appropriate on the first interview, but by the second or third interview with the company, I'd try to schedule it for first thing in the morning. Generally people are less rushed and distracted.

I'd suggest your student try to get the morning appointment and then bring in a dozen donuts and offer it to the staff person who greets him or her.

Remember part of the decision process hangs on – "Will they fit in with the culture?" A $7 box of donuts can swing the deal and position your student to negotiate for another $1,000 in salary!

But you need to remind your student that the interview process does not stop at the interview, and should continue in a well organized follow up plan that includes:

1. Sending a written thank you note to the interviewer

2. Following up in writing with information the interviewer indicated they would like to see

3. Periodic emails that provide additional evidence of their capability that can include testimonials, projects, blog articles and/or awards

Most interviewees walk away thinking they hit it out of the park, but they need to be reminded that the interviewers spend their day meeting people and more than likely their interview will be boiled down to some text on a piece of paper that will lose its luster within hours.

The follow up and continued communication over a period of weeks that reminds the interviewer of your student's strong points and that includes a photo will help your student stay on the hiring manager's short list!

KNOWING WHERE TO SEARCH

Looking for a job today is SO different than looking even 5 years ago.

The job seeker today has access to so much more information that was not available in the past. This information will help him or her identify:

- Jobs before they are posted

- Contracts being awarded that will likely result in new hires

- Mergers of companies that could result in expansions

- Companies moving to a new location which will result in hiring

- People working within desirable companies that he or she can contact

In fact, there is so much opportunity for job seekers to control their job search process that didn't exist in the past and the sad thing is that few grads or experienced workers have a clue about how to use them.

Think about it.

In the past, when you were looking for jobs, you had your network that you communicated with via phone, water cooler and classified ads. Today you have:

- LinkedIn

- Facebook

- Twitter

- Blogs

- Google Alerts

- Job boards

- Company and industry e-newsletters

as well as numerous other sources like Bloomburg, WSJ, all TV networks, Plaxo, Spokeo and many more!

Unfortunately, these have all come online so fast, most of us have not been able to understand how we can use these free resources to get jobs.

When your student creates a job profile and job search plan he or she will begin laying out a foundation including an analysis of which of these tools and services they want to include in their job search plan.   Now they need the skills and knowledge about how to use these effectively. They will need to know the easiest ways to research companies, opportunities, and changes in industries, to find out about companies and networks so they can have "first mover advantage," and how to then leverage that advantage with their personal network to gain immediate introductions.

It's part science, part art, but it requires a change in one's behavior.

I can guarantee you that your student does not have a clue about how to incorporate these tools and build a comprehensive strategy that will automatically deliver the news and information he or she needs, when it is needed.

You are going to have to encourage your student to pick up the skills and knowledge about how to do this research.

As part of his or her daily plan, your student should be setting aside time to:

1. Read relevant career and industry blogs, as well as eNewsletters

2. Check their LinkedIn, Facebook, Twitter and other news feeds for chatter and relevant news

3. Read daily news feeds from online bulletin boards

4. Research the companies that traditionally hire students from his or her school and connect with those firms' fan pages to get news updates

5. Talk to career center staff, deans and faculty members to ask for leads of companies that might be hiring

6. Look for companies who are offering internships to graduated students

7. Identify volunteer opportunities they can start on immediately in order to add work experience and show initiative

There are a couple ways to make this process easier.

I would strongly suggest your student set up a Google Alert account which will enable your student to track companies, industries and/or any keyword that is relevant to his or her job search. By doing that each day your student will receive a list of blogs, tweets, press releases and/or updates on websites that relate to that keyword.

For example, I might receive an update that indicates Monsanto, a firm I want to work for, just got a new contract with the government. I could then go to my contacts that I know at Monsanto and congratulate them, plus go to their fan page and also congratulate the company.

Remember, getting jobs has a lot to do with being at the right place and the right time and the more a face is in front of its intended audience, the greater chance the person will get a job with the firm they want at the salary and benefits he or she deserves.

7) Build a professional network

Mark Granovetter, a sociologist at Stanford University is well known for his research on interpersonal relationships and networks.

Mark was among the first experts to prove that the most effective way to get a job is through networking. His research showed that approximately 80% of job seekers get jobs through friends and friends of their friends.

Granovetter's research suggests the need to build a network that reaches beyond people that we interact with on a daily basis because statistically our closest connections produce the smallest number of job placements.

His research showed that:

- Moderate ties are the people you interact with weekly, which represent 55% of one's contacts.

- Weak ties are the people you interact with monthly, which represent 22% of one's contacts.

- Strong ties are family members, classmates and friends, which represent 17% ones contacts.

This analysis shows that your student has to reach a wide variety of people and actually concentrate on connections OF connections if he or she wants to increase his or her chances of getting a job. Essentially, your student needs to be concentrating on weak and moderate ties like:

- Barbers, bakers, local business owners, and even your neighbors

- Members of your church that are spread throughout the community

- People you meet at health clubs, events etc.

...and alumni!

The research shows that people you have some kind of relationship with or something in common with can be very valuable in the job search. That's why connecting with alumni should be at the center of a networking strategy.

Alumni share the traditions, clubs, courses and activities your student will be participating in. While they are students, they will have an extra edge in being able to connect with alumni. After students graduate, the acceptance rate, particularly with alumni at higher positions, will diminish.

If we had our way, your student would be building an alumni network before he or she even entered college. As he or she begins looking for a college, your student needs to create a LinkedIn profile and search for alumni from that college who are in the career path in which your student is interested.

Once they find these connections, your student should request an opportunity to connect so he or she can ask a few questions. They might say something like:

> "Hi, XXX, I'm considering going to XXXX college and noticed you graduated in the same major; I was hoping I might be able to connect with you to ask you a few questions about the department and for some suggestions you might have for me."

Then once a connection has accepted your student's request, he or she might say something like:

1. What activities, curriculum, events did you think were most valuable in building your career strategy?

2. What clubs and organizations would you recommend being a part of that would help prepare for a career in this industry?

3. Would you be willing to introduce me (the student) to other alumni?

4. What would you have done differently to prepare for this career while in college?

When students make their final selections of colleges, they need to immediately find 5-8 alumni who have majors and minors in the areas of the students' interests. They need to periodically connect with these insiders during their freshman years, not only to provide moments for their mentors to reminisce, but to also ask for advice about courses, clubs, activities --all the while learning more about their mentors.

Ideally, they will have at 5-6 contacts with the alumni mentors during the school year and a couple of contacts during the summer. Remind your student that their mentors need to get something out of these relationships, too.

Your student could:

1. Give them updates on faculty and start discussions where the mentor could share memories from their time on campus.

2. Share with them the list of upcoming speakers and/or campus visitors.

3. Provide a heads up on a crisis, issue or major event that is occurring on campus.

4. Remind the mentor if he or she coming in for homecoming that they'd be happy to show the mentor around the "new" places to be seen or have a drink.

5. Send a small token or gift from the college. Many times the alumni association or admissions office has things they give away, mugs, banners, key chains etc. Your student could stop by and collect a series of things for their mentors.

You get the idea?

The dialogue and discussion has to change each year. The **sophomore year** is a time to start cashing in on the contacts and industry knowledge. The goal this year is to get as much help as possible to find relevant internships. The investment your student made in developing a relationship the first year will pan out, as now he or she has the alum invested in his or her success. The mentor will want to help as much as possible. So now your student needs to be:

• Asking for more introductions of friends, and/or other alumni who are in the same career path, so your student can make contact for possible internships

- Sharing a resume and ramping up the LinkedIn profile so the alumni and his or her contacts can effortlessly share it with others

- Periodically offering evidence of projects your student is working on, books your student is reading that are relevant to the industry, and/or a blog your student started related to his or her career interests etc.

- Continuing to keep the mentor(s) vested in, proud of, and knowledgeable about his or her capabilities will give them incentive to tout your student to contacts and peers

During the **junior year**, your student should be trying to get opportunities to job shadow the mentors. He or she should consider asking for an opportunity to visit with a mentor for a couple hours or even for a full day to get a perspective of what the contact does. Most mentors will try to build this visit on a day when he or she will have a series of meetings, and/or activities that will give the student a better understanding of what a typical day might look like. This will be important for your student as he or she will not only learn what he or she likes, but what he or she doesn't want to do.

By the **senior year,** hopefully your student has built a strong enough relationship with his/her mentors that these contacts are doing lots of work to help your student get a job. Assuming your student has kept his or her mentors aware of how he or she is doing with class projects, grades and extracurricular activities, and is providing something back to the mentors, it will be easier for mentors to not only sell them but to want to spend the time to help your student find a job, because your student deserves it.

Your student's relationship with mentors should be a two way street. Mentors like to talk about themselves and of course share real world experience. Students need to spend 70 percent of the time learning about the mentor so they can really get to know and respect what these mentors are about to offer them. That involves asking questions. Students will need to know things like:

- What did you do when you first got out of college?

- What kind of preparation and experience did you need?

- What would you have done differently?

- What was the biggest issue you faced as you started your career?

- What job or responsibility did you enjoy most?

- What did you do to adapt to corporate life?

- What do companies look for in a person in order to consider them for advancement?

- What is the typical career path out of this position?

Building a two way relationship will enrich both the student and the mentor.

NETWORKING AT EVENTS

I remember the first event I went to after I graduated from college. Even though I loved marketing, I had little experience in it so after graduating I thought it might be a good idea to join a marketing group or association. I noticed the local chapter of the American Marketing Association was meeting at a hotel near me. I decided to go. When I arrived and stepped into the room, I immediately panicked as everyone seemed to be paired in conversation and, being naturally shy, I turned and left!

Fortunately, as I developed my photography business I needed to pick up marketing skills in order to reach businesses and consumers, so I returned to these meetings, met great people, learned a lot, and built some lifelong friendships.

Going to events like this will help your student overcome shyness too!

The Stanford Shyness Clinic's research shows that 60% of us consider ourselves shy. The majority would never consider speaking in front of an audience and dread having to introduce ourselves in group settings.

Many schools and colleges are doing a good job today encouraging students to speak in front of the class. This still remains an area where all of us need nudging and encouragement to get involved and engaged in these groups.

Why?

Because groups love younger members!

New and youthful members are looked at as potential future leaders of the groups and it adds new perspective and life to groups. Remind your student that he or she will be welcomed!

What kind of events and activities should your student go to?

1. Alumni events. It doesn't matter if it's a tailgate party, fundraising event or gathering of buddies, alumni events are important to stay engaged as the alumni network is strong and wide!

2. Associations and get togethers within communities. Nearly every profession has a national organization that holds local meetings-- PR, marketing, sales, engineers, accountants, nurses, everyone! With a bit of research and a few dollars for a membership fee, a world of new contacts opens up to your student.

3. Conferences related to the industry. Many conferences offer students free access and graduates discounted registration fees.

4. LinkedIn events are held in cities across the nation. Have your student look for LinkedIn (name of your town) and they'll meet a cross section of new and interesting people they can add to their network.

5. MeetUp is an online tool where people and groups organize meet-ups based on interests, hobbies and/or events. This doesn't have to be business related. 5 years ago I joined the Beatles Meet-up in Akron, Ohio just to find people who liked similar music. Often in these events your student will build new relationships that could lead to future jobs.

Networking experts like Diane Darling author of *The Networking Survival Guide* reminds us that we need to go to events like these with a purpose. We need to remember that networking is an engaged sport, one in which we first find "what value we can provide" to those we meet and then, follow up on it so we can build trust and credibility when we need to ask them for help.

If your student has not taken the time to learn networking skills either by a course or books like Diane's, encourage him or her to do so. Virtually NO ONE knows how to professionally network. It's a learned sport.

Only a small percentage of us are born networkers and even those have few skills concerning how to manage the networking process in order to benefit all parties. Networking skills, in my opinion, are among the most important your student will need to not only launch and maintain a successful career, but to also enrich his or her life by meeting fascinating people who share the same interests, hobbies and personal goals.

SUMMARY

So there you have it-- 7 fundamental building blocks that will help your graduate build a successful career and life!

We see you having enormous influence on this process. If YOU don't require it – it WILL NOT happen!

Don't expect your student to pick up each area and take off running. As you can see, there is a lot of information that both you and your student need to adjust to. Based on what you know about your student, pick the suggestions you know your student can adjust to and adapt to the fastest first – then move on to the next!

COMING UP!

Now that you know how much the employment landscape has changed and the difficulty your student will face in securing his or her first job, we'll show you proven techniques about how your student can stand out from others!

In the business world, everyone is paid in two coins: cash and experience. Take the experience first; the cash will come later.

- Harold Geneen, Past President of ATT

YOUR TO DO'S AND NOTES!

CHAPTER RESOURCES

8

12 GUERILLA MARKETING TECHNIQUES
THAT GET JOBS

Now you'll learn about our favorite, proven strategies that will help your graduate standout, get interviews and jobs!

With the average human resource manager now having to wade through hundreds of resumes, your student really has to do something EXTRAORDINARY to stand out!

We have talked about using keywords that related to the job position so your student's resume will have a better chance of being sorted to the top of the stack and have discussed dozens of other ways of using online communities and social media to get noticed.

Now we are going to talk about techniques and ideas that collectively, and/or individually will give yours student an opportunity to stand out from the crowd.

I'm not advocating that your son or daughter implement all of these techniques, but that he or she finds techniques which fit his or her personality, interests and skills and then stick with those.

All your student really needs is one idea or one technique to stand out. Heck it could be something as simple as the way he or she dresses!

Recently I attended an event held by the Northeast Ohio Council on Internships where Ohio State University President, Gordon Gee, spoke. For as long as I can remember (and that goes back 20 years) I've seen President Gee nearly a dozen times at conventions, graduations, and events and he always has a bow tie on. He's not alone. Others who have been known to wear bow ties include:

- Steve Jobs

- Winston Churchill

- Orville Redenbacher

- Louis Farrakhan

Entertainers are also well known for wearing clothes, tattoos and/or jewelry to stand out.

I was in Washington D.C. walking to an appointment a number of years ago when I saw across the street Matthew Lesko, an author and self-proclaimed federal grant researcher and infomercial personality. I'd seen Lesko on late night TV commercials telling me how to get "free" money from the U.S. government. The way he caught my attention on TV was with his custom made suits with question marks (???) all over them.

On that bright sunny Thursday afternoon in Washington, D.C., I realized Matthew's "Riddler" like suit was not made just for TV - as there he was standing on the corner donning his question mark suit! Man did that catch my attention! Although I've never purchased his products, I've never forgotten his angle. It became obvious that he made his dress part of his personal brand.

I'm not suggesting your student walk into an interview with the company's logo all over a suit, or that he or she dress up as the company's mascot for an interview (might be cute though), but I am suggesting that they find creative ways to make an impression!

THERE ARE OTHER WAYS TO GET NOTICED!

Dianez Smith offers a variation on Lesko's technique.

During the peak Washington, D.C. morning rush hour commute, the 26 year old graduate from Arcadia University stood at the corner of K and 17th street at 6:00 a.m. holding a large handmade sign that said: "I am a recent graduate searching for employment -- resume available."

Dianez was looking for an opportunity to break out of working at a bike shop where she was paid $8 an hour, and find a job where she could use her degree to start a career. Her savvy guerilla marketing worked, as she was offered a job starting as a receptionist and junior legal assistant at a firm only a few doors down from where she was standing!

Hmm... Now that I think of it, it might be one way to get the attention of people within a company they want to work for. I could see someone standing outside a business that says, "I want to work for your company, let me be part of your solutions! I come with a personal guarantee."

There are dozens of strategies your student can adopt that will keep him or her focused and will give your student an edge over others.

Let's look at 12 of my favorite strategies:

1. The Alumni Connection

2. Try before you buy

3. Hidden job market

4. Apply for positions of people who just got jobs

5. Find a problem and offer a solution

6. Marketing and advertising

7. Five calls a day

8. Hang out

9. Drip Marketing

10. Control the Interview

11. The Post Card

12. Build "thought leadership"

1) The Alumni Connection

We've covered some of this in earlier parts of the book, but I'm including it here because of any strategy, this is by far the easiest, carries the least risk, and frankly, it's fun to be able to connect with alumni of all ages!

The alumni connection is the most powerful internship, job and business generating strategy available to graduates and alumni. Your student will not find a more supportive group of people. These are people that walked the same paths, attended the same lectures, lived in the same dorms and suffered through the same food! They will be supportive, encouraging and will go out of their ways to help.

As good a technique as this is, surprisingly few graduates take advantage of it.

Graduates from Harvard realize this. In 1998, when my firm was creating online communities for alumni associations around the world, I attended a local event on entrepreneurship and started talking to an attendee that happened to be a Harvard graduate. I shared with him what I did and he mentioned he used his alumni online community frequently to find fellow grads with expertise, knowledge, resources and/or interests in doing business deals.

He went on to say one of the reasons a student will choose Harvard is they understand they are joining a network of alumni who understand the value of networking and that the network will introduce them to business and life opportunities they would never get from other institutions.

Years later, the house next door to me was bought by a Harvard graduate. Corrine and I were having coffee one morning when I mentioned I'd love to get some articles in the Huffington Post. While we were talking she searched her Blackberry for a name (keep in mind this was 7:15 am), and proceeded to call a fellow Harvard alum, who within 15 minutes called back with the steps I needed to take to get an article in the Huffington Post.

Harvard graduates get it.

Corrine reminded me that this situation happens because she stays in touch with her network. She periodically connects with them to find out how things are going, asks them what they are working on and what's happening in their lives. To develop a network, one has to not only care about the people he or she is networking with, but get to know those people in their lives, the issues they face, and their achievements.

Unfortunately, most colleges do not inculcate this into their classes or curriculum, nor do they build this into the culture of the students and alumni.

Very early in my career of building alumni online communities I called Texas A&M. I reached their 800 number and a recording said, "Welcome to the Texas A&M Alumni Association. Your Alumni Association is your professional network of over 200,000 professionals," and I thought, "These guys really get it."

It doesn't matter if your student is graduating from an Ivy League, state, private or even community college, an alum is an alum, and every single one will go out of his or her way to help a fellow alum.

But, you will have to get your student to develop this network early.

They need to be working it the day they arrive on campus and continue working it until they retire. It was nearly impossible for students to connect with alumni even a decade ago. There wasn't an effective way to do so. The alumni association might have had a 3-ring binder that listed alumni interested in mentoring students, but even then students had to come to the alumni association to connect with them.

Today, students don't need the alumni association to broker relationships, they can do it by themselves on LinkedIn, Facebook, Plaxo, Branchout and to a very limited degree on the official alumni online community.

To be effective at networking with alumni your student will need:

1. A 30 second elevator pitch
2. The ability to differentiate himself or herself
3. To be helpful to the network
4. To know how to approach alumni
5. To be clear about what he or she wants
6. To follow up
7. To show gratitude

We recommend your student join the LinkedIn alumni group and search for alumni who:

- Live in the same geographical area
- Work at companies in which your student shows interest
- Have similar majors
- Are part of the same groups
- Went to college during the same time

Refer back to the discussion we had about creating an online identity for more details about how to specifically use LinkedIn and Facebook to build networks.

2) Try before you buy!

I was talking to a human resource manager recently because I wanted him to be a part of our upcoming webinars. He was an author and noted expert.

During our conversation he said, "Don, what it really comes down to is this. What's the number one thing hiring managers fear?" I paused, and said, "Hiring the wrong candidate?" and he said "Right."

He went on and said, "In my opinion you can take all the books, all the hiring advice, and information and set it aside if you adopt one strategy."

What he said next just about floored me because it made so much sense!

> "My advice to any job seeker is to really do their homework and find out what they want to do, then look for job opportunities and zero in on the ones they really want to do. They need to do whatever it takes to get in for an interview and in that interview, offer to fill the position for 30 days at no pay with no obligation, and with no strings attached."

I think he has a great point.

By offering a "No Obligation – Personal Guarantee" the company has no risk and will be able to determine if the person is the right fit in the company culture, and if he or she has the right knowledge, creativity and work ethic the company needs.

A couple months later, my best friend Nick and I were checking off one of the things on our "bucket lists" by participating in the 40-mile Five Borough New York Bike Tour. It's an incredibly cool event where some 30,000 people start at Wall Street, right next to Ground Zero, and ride through all 5 boroughs of New York City. You go past Wall Street, through Manhattan, Central Park, the Bronx, Queens, Brooklyn and then over the Verrazano bridge, ending up in Staten Island.

It's really a fun experience.

Instead of staying in New York City, we stayed with Nick's mother in the home she and her husband bought in Wayne, New Jersey to raise their 3 boys some 40 years ago. Yia-ya, now 83, is one of the best cooks to come across the ocean from Greece. Nick turned into a teenager with a ravenous appetite when she pulled out his favorite "mom" dishes.

She's a fascinating woman that has a story we can relate to all of our kids.

Yia-ya had a comfortable life in Greece but longed to move to America at age 17. So after World War II, she-- like millions of Europeans-- risked everything to come to America.

While Nick and I were busy eating a fabulous dinner, Yia-ya shared what she did to get her first job. It was exactly the advice the executive I just mentioned shared with me.

Yia-ya visited a company she wanted to work at, but she had no experience. She approached the hiring manager and told him she wanted to work for free the first month, and after that - if they thought she could do the job, they could hire her full time.

I'm sure the hiring manager was still trying to process what she had said when she made one more request. She told him that she wanted to use her own tools. After he picked himself off the floor, he called in his boss and repeated what Yia-ya had said. Of course, neither of them had ever heard this before or had been offered this kind of deal. It definitely set them back and I'm sure they talked about it for years!

Of course she got the job and along with her husband's salary, they raised and supported three hungry boys!

So it works… and it has worked for generations.

Now that I think of it, a friend from grade school through high school did that too!

Randy Pfund was a star athlete in football and basketball at Wheaton North High School and later at Wheaton College where he averaged 25 points a game in basketball. I moved from Wheaton at the end of my junior year and lost track of Randy and the rest of the kids I grew up with.

Twenty years later when the class was planning its 20th reunion and we were all reconnecting, one of my best friends in junior high and high school, Larry Mandel, shared Randy's amazing story with me.

Soon after graduating from high school, Randy got a job teaching history and coaching at Glenbard South High School. Randy, like the rest of us, really didn't have a career plan in place. At 23 years of age, his main desire to teach was to enable him to buy a car - so that he did not have to rely on his buddies to get him around town.

While attending the 1977 NCAA basketball championship tournament in Atlanta with his father, then a retired basketball coach for Wheaton College, Randy got inspired. According to Randy, "Marquette was playing North Carolina in the final game. The intensity of the game, the passions of the fans, and the excitement that enveloped the game were overwhelming. I realized at that moment, that I wanted to coach a college basketball team."

Long before email, the Internet and cell phones, Randy did what every job seeker did in those days, he wrote 30 letters to colleges across the country looking for an opportunity to coach. One by one, 29 colleges responded with letters notifying him that they did not have a position open at the time.

Finally, a letter arrived from Westmont College in Santa Barbara, California. Chet Kammerer the head basketball coach offered Randy an opportunity to coach, but Chet indicated he didn't have a budget to pay him a salary.

He'd have to work for free!

It's not quite the offer you can't refuse, but, then there was the lure of California in the late 1970's, the chance to fulfill his dream, and to get out of town. Randy cashed in what little he had in his teacher's retirement fund and headed west.

Randy cut his teeth coaching at Westmont College for seven years. (Yes, they did eventually pay him - but not a lot!) He subsidized his income by scouting basketball players for Bill Bertka. After proving himself, Bill introduced Randy to Pat Riley, then the head coach of the Los Angeles Lakers. Pat was impressed with Randy and in 1985 asked him to join the Lakers as an assistant coach. Not only did Randy get a chance to coach a college basketball team, but now he was coaching on one of the greatest teams in the history of basketball!

But, the story doesn't end there.

After nearly a thousand games with the Lakers, Randy was promoted to head coach from 1992 through 1994.

Randy's willingness to work for free took him well beyond his dreams when the Lakers won two National Basketball championships while he was on the coaching staff. If that wasn't enough to cap a successful career, Randy went on to become the General Manager of the Miami Heat where his experience, recruitment acumen and industry knowledge helped lead the team to a NBA championship in 2005!

If your student is out looking for a job and he or she sees something they really would like to do, would it hurt to try this technique?

It's not like they just stepped off the boat from Europe like Yia-ya. You'll be there for your student making sure he or she has a roof overhead and food to eat!

Like Randy, they could very likely go beyond their dreams and expectations.

IT ACTUALLY HELPS COMPANIES

Many companies will spend 6 months to a full year filling a position.

If a graduate approaches them early on, he or she can offer to fill the position until they complete the hiring phase and if they find a better candidate, that's ok, the graduate will be able to share the experience and their willingness to work on their resume.

The drawback is your student will have to be in a situation where they can work for free for the designated period of time. If they were already living at home, and had no job during that time period, they really didn't lose any money.

Depending on the company, I might suggest they consider negotiating a sign up bonus if the company is happy with the results. Consider asking for ½ a month pay to receive as compensation for the work done.

3) Look for positions of people who just got jobs

In the 12-Hour Grad Career Marathon we hold every June, Mark Gonska, Senior Vice President and Career Coach for Dise and Company shared an incredible strategy with grads that bears repeating.

While the idea is not one that a grad is going to use for a first job, it's probably one he or she can employ the rest of his or her life. Mark reminds us that everyone that is hired is more than likely leaving a similar position at another firm. Let's assume your student is in the final three but doesn't get the job.

While talking with the hiring manager, your student should ask for the name of the person they hired and what company that person worked for. If the hiring manager is not in a position to give that information, Mark suggests checking the Linkedin profile of the person who got hired. All of us list the firms we work and of course all your student will have to do is click on the old company website listing and talk to the hiring manager.

If that doesn't work, he suggests making a call later-- after first the position has been hired-- and talk with a receptionist to get that information.

Mark has personally used this technique a number of times in his business career and it seems as relevant of an idea today as ever.

This is a great idea for anyone looking for a job!

4) The Hidden Job Market

Donald Asher, author of the book, *Cracking the Hidden Job Market* shared information at one of our Grad Career Webinars on how students can get jobs through the hidden job market. Donald shares a number of proven strategies in his book and defines the hidden job market as representing something between 55% and 80% of all open jobs.

That's big! In fact he goes on to say:

- About 2/3 of people who take a new position did not respond to an opening posted on the internet or anywhere else for that matter.

- About 2/3 of hiring takes place through people to people conversations.

- Almost all of the hidden job market is driven by personal interaction.

- Only 2/3 of all jobs are ever advertised online.

- More than ½ of all hiring is through the hidden job market.

The great things about concentrating on the hidden job market is:

- There are less people vying for the position.

- You get first mover opportunity to make an impression.

...and it's easier!

By now you know that 80 percent of us get jobs through people we know. Most of the time these jobs are already posted and the HR department is actively advertising them. However, there are other situations where a candidate can either create a job for himself or herself, or get in before a job is even posted.

- Every company has problems or issues they haven't solved, but need to create a position to handle.

- Some companies suspend looking for a candidate because they cannot find the right candidate or management gets burned out, and the process stops.

- Timing is everything! As the economy improves, employees will become more mobile and chances are you can find a position available because someone just resigned.

- If you are watching the company press releases, watch for new contracts the company wins as it could indicate they will need to start hiring

There are a number of ways to learn about the hidden job market:

- Set up a Google Alert for the company to watch announcements about the firm.

- Follow the company on LinkedIn which will give you alerts of new hires and/or jobs posted through the LinkedIn channel.

- Follow the company blog, HR Twitter account, or those of people within targeted departments.

- And of course, just make phone calls!

During phone calls to friends, family members and managers of departments, your grad should ask them if they have had any projects that have been stalled due to lack of attention. As a way of building a relationship with the firm, and giving them an opportunity to see his or her talents, a job seeker could offer to do a short term stint for the company to get the project up and running.

5) Find a problem and offer a solution.

Companies today need to be constantly looking for problems they can solve for their customers.

Many companies have so many initiatives going on they can barely keep track of them. Inevitably there are so many day-to-day responsibilities and crises that arise that it's nearly impossible for companies to keep their "improvement" initiatives moving forward.

In a number of chapters in this book, we've advocated that your student connect on LinkedIn with people in the companies he or she wants to work for. Your student's number one objective is to get to know people in the company, and for the company employees to get to know your student. Your graduate will want to share the events, clubs, activities and leadership positions he or she has participated in, but at the same time he or she should be making periodic contacts with insiders to find out how things are going at the company.

Your student should be asking questions like:

- Are there any new projects happening in your department and/ or company?

   o   How is that going?

- What issues are you, and/or your department and company currently facing?

- In any recent meetings have there been any projects that keep getting stalled because staff hasn't had the time to complete research or action items?

- What would you like to do in your position or department that you've not had the time to accomplish?

The answers to these questions will help give your student an opportunity to propose to the contact either an internship, or entry level position that will help the company complete these initiatives and those that haven't made it to the white board yet.

After collecting this information your student should tell the contact he or she is going to put together a quick one page proposal that will identify how he or she can help the company complete these tasks. Assuming the contact thinks it would be a good idea, your student should get a commitment to provide feedback and introduce it at the next meeting.

I can guarantee you there isn't a company out there today that doesn't have action items and projects that are stalled due to employees not having the time, or taking the time, to complete them.

This is an incredibly easy way for your student to work his or her way into a position without even interviewing.

I promise you, companies are looking for creative, passionate and action oriented people. If this technique doesn't get your student an immediate opportunity, I can guarantee it will make an impression and when something does become available – he or she will get a call.

6) Marketing and advertising

LinkedIn and Facebook are giving entrepreneurial grads an opportunity to be found by hiring managers, people and companies who they would be interested in working for.

It's really a neat idea and one that can be done on a shoe string budget.

Let's consider Facebook first, because it will probably be the easiest and least expensive way for your graduate try this out. In fact, Facebook's advertising system is so easy it would take your graduate as little as 5 minutes to create an ad they could target by:

- Location
- College
- Company

- Interests

- Connections

- Age

So, for example, your graduate could create a series of ads to reach people within a company they are interested in.

- He or she could target people who are under 30 and working for the company, and run an ad that might say, "New grad from XXXX really wants to work at XXXX company."

- Another group might be individuals working at the company with a specific title. Perhaps it's Vice President. The ad might say, "XXXX Company – I've got skills to increase your profits!"

- Yet another might be an ad targeted to people within the company that have similar interests. Their ad might look like this, "You love photography, I love photography and I want to work for you!"

Your student can run a series of ads and set a daily budget of as little as a couple dollars a day to reach this group. When someone clicks on the ad, Facebook enables the advertisers to drive the person wherever the advertiser wants to take them. So your student might take the viewer to a personal profile page, a personal website or even a LinkedIn page.

LinkedIn also gives companies and individuals the ability to advertise on their platform, although it's more expensive. Your graduate would have similar flexibility and the ability to advertise, like with Facebook-- right down to a specific person. <u>Meaning that if the only person you wanted to reach was a hiring manager, you could do that</u>. Anytime he or she was on the site, your student would have the opportunity to drive an ad to that person.

Want a real example?

Matthew Epstein used video in his pitch for a product marketing position at Google. The 24 year old spent nearly two months looking for jobs through the traditional channels but ended up with no leads. So he invested $3,000 from his savings and created a marketing campaign called, googlepleasehire.me

He created a 4 minute video staged in a historic mansion that featured Epstein sipping Scotch and speaking to the camera about why he was the right person for the job. He put the video on a page that included Why Google and About Me sections and listed 10 reasons why Google should hire him.

He started promoting his video and page through his 200 Facebook friends and 100 Twitter followers. His followers shared with their networks and by that evening he was receiving job interviews from around the country.

It worked...but not with Google!

The job he took was not with Google, but with SigFig, a San Francisco based financial startup. The CEO of the company thought his creativity and entrepreneurial attitude was what their firm needed.

Pretty neat stuff, frankly very easy to do, and believe me, not many people are taking advantage of this.

7) Ten - 15 calls a day and thank you notes

As part of their daily regime your student should be making outbound calls to connect with companies they are interested in working for and building relationships with hiring managers. In today's voice mail dominated society it's tough to get through to people. In fact, it will more than likely take your student 10 calls to reach 1 person live.

There are a couple strategies in making daily phone calls:

- Call to find out if there are any positions available

- Call to follow up on correspondence

- Building relationships

- Follow ups on interviews

Calls are an important part of the job search because it gives your student an opportunity to get in front of people, test out an elevator pitch, and build listening skills and interviewing skills.

However, few students feel like calls are necessary. They've been weaned on instant chat, email and texting. Encourage them to set aside an

<u>hour a day to make cold calls to companies they are interested in and later to make follow up calls.</u>

Now the next step is very important.

Depending on the type of call, if the person your student talked to offered a suggestion, lead, or idea, your graduate should consider sending him or her a thank you card.   Thank you cards can be picked up at the local drug store for less than $5 for a bundle of 25. These will be worth their weights in gold in their return on investment.

All your student has to do is jot down a quick note thanking the contact for taking their call and sharing the idea, lead or tip and indicate he or she will follow up on it.   According to Diane Darling, author of "Networking Survival Guide":

> "In this data driven, email saturated world, a Thank You card stands out and has a long shelf live because the recipient remembers it.   It's one of the more powerful – traditional – techniques available to individuals who are interested in building a network in which all parties take away something."

8) Hang out with people they want to work for

This generation has so many advantages to look for jobs that you did not have.

They have incredible access to working professionals at levels that were unheard of when you were looking for your first jobs. You couldn't access CEO's, presidents, or heads of organizations with the ease social media sites offer.

LinkedIn is one of the new tools that enables your student to reach to the top of the corporate ladder with the ease of a few clicks and never have to pick up a phone or send a letter.

LinkedIn gives your graduate the opportunity to hang out with business professionals and participate in discussions whenever they want. LinkedIn Groups have been formed by literally every profession and can have hundreds of thousands of members or as few as 100. Your student should be finding groups of people in the industries they want to work in – and then hang out and participate.

Frankly, that's the easy part.

All your student has to do is look at the bottom of the page of the people with whom he or she wants to connect. The profile page will list the names of LinkedIn Groups the contact is a part of. With this information they can go to the Group search box, find the group and join.

Once your student is a member of that group, he or she can jump in on conversations and discussions. I've seen students inform members that they are students, which immediately puts members of the group on notice to take a nurturing and supportive role. As a member of the group, students will also be able to follow people who are making comments and offering ideas and advice.

For a generation that is focused on their iPhones, iPads and computers, this will be a fun way for them to build connections and their brands 24/7.

9) Drip Marketing

Advertisers know it takes as many as 6 exposures to their ads to get your attention.

This doesn't mean you are going to go out and buy the product immediately, but studies show by the 6th exposure, chances are you will finally pay attention to their ad and will be influenced by their brand and messaging in the future.

Your student is going to need to do the same thing, but with the dozens of people who he or she is connecting with. To effectively use drip marketing, your graduate could build a strategy that delivers his or her message across multiple marketing channels including online, offline, via phone, mail or in person.

There are numerous free tools available that can accommodate and organize this process for your student. One of my favorite organizational ideas to deliver a series of emails designed to keep your student in front of hiring managers is a free email marketing tool called MailChimp.

MailChimp will enable your student to set up Autoresponders that are essentially an automated way to send emails to targeted people. Your student can set up 1, 5 or dozens of emails.

The first thing your student needs to do is create a strategy about what he or she wants to say, cover and review. For example:

- A first email might be a thank you for taking a moment to connect with the student.

- Next, your student may want to point to his or her personal blog or personal website that provides additional information about himself or herself.

- It also might make sense to share a personal success story and a link to your student's LinkedIn page.

Once your student has identified what he or she wants to cover and writes a script, the next thing to do is to decide what kind of additional tools he or she can use to stand out. For example, in a 3rd email your student may want to include a link to a video bio where he or she can answer questions about himself or herself to give the hiring manager an idea of whether he or she is a good fit for the company and how he or she may handle customers.

Or, if the positions your student is applying for are more on the creative side, your student may direct the recipient to a Flickr account to see photos of art, graphic design and other projects.

The idea is to put in place a creative series of emails that are not repetitive, but informative, and provide the student's message in a variety of formats. When your student's creativity comes across – it will provide him or her a huge advantage.

MailChimp and other products like it enable your student to personalize each email and deliver the emails according to any scheduled time frame. For example, when your student adds my name to his or her database, he or she can trigger the email to go out the next day and then every week, month or quarter to send another email. The system is smart enough to deliver and keep everyone's emails on schedule and all your student has to do is add the new contact information and forget about it.

Your student can start with 1 or 100 contacts and continue to add to them as they meet more people. It's a great way to use technology and make connections that think your student has been thinking of them.

Timing in a job search is everything and your student needs to understand that no response from a hiring managers is not always, "No!" The manager may have an offer out to someone and be waiting for that person to make a decision. People refuse jobs all the time because:

- The pay may be too low.

- Their spouse decided they didn't want to move.

- One of their other opportunities or current employer made a better offer.

- They failed a drug test.

- Their credit and background check failed.

It's not unusual for the company to have to go through 1, 2 or even to a third choice before it gets a viable candidate. Keeping a slow stream of positive, informative information keeps your student in the game.

One other advantage of tools like these is that your student will be able to determine who opened and/or clicked to view additional information. It will give them an idea of which of their connections is engaged with the information. I'd use this information to determine which ones to call from time to time.

10) Control the Interview

One of the presenters for the free webinars we offer to over 1000 career centers, Eric Kramer, has a technique called *Active Interviewing*.

Eric reminds us in his book called, *Active Interviewing,* that most hiring managers are not professional interviewers and have little human resource training.

With 99 percent of business in America considered small business, hiring managers are stepping out of their day to day roles of running the company and squeezing in the time to interview candidates. Most do not have formal training and nearly all have no clue about how to conduct an interview. The frightening thing about this is the best candidate can be passed over because the person responsible for hiring the position in a department was distracted and did not see the diamond sitting right in front of him or her.

So Eric recommends job seekers create a presentation that guides the interviewer through their qualifications, achievements and experience. It's really a brilliant idea as it puts less pressure on the interviewer to dig for information and then to try to retain it. Eric recommends each presentation be customized for each interview in order to have the greatest impact. Many of his clients use PowerPoint to create a series of slides that answer the background, experience, qualifications, etc. questions that need to be covered.

The presentation should include:

- Awards/Testimonials
- Leadership positions
- Stats
- Blogs, Twitter
- Example of reports
- Creativity
- Desire for learning

Once the presentation is finished, two copies can be printed and taken to the interview.

At an appropriate time in the interview, your student would say something like, "I've produced a presentation that will give you a good idea of my qualifications and how they fit in the position you are looking to fill - may I share it with you?" According to Eric, only rarely will they get a negative response. This might occur in larger firms that have tight schedules and ridged interviewing requirements.

But according to Eric, this really works!

11) The post card

Author Donald Asher has a unique approach to help your student stand out in the job search process.

Donald works with hiring managers and knows how busy they are. They have less than one minute to review a resume and certainly don't have the time to reach back to candidates with rejection letters or letters with advice. His technique makes it easier for the hiring manager to give the candidate additional feedback and advice on who they might contact and with whom to share additional information.

He suggests they send a post card along with their cover letter and resume or as part of their drip marketing campaign that has a postage paid stamp on it and prewritten questions that require a quick fill in of a name, phone number or of simply a check mark.

It's a powerful and easy way to keep the relationship going and to be redirected to information or people needed to get a job at that organization.

You can make your own post card by simply giving the person the ability to fill in a check mark for:

- We haven't made a decision yet

- We've filled the position

- Please contact me

Or pick up Donald's book to pick up a few more secrets and recommendations on how to make this technique work for you!

12) Develop Thought Leadership

Your first question is, "What the heck is thought leadership?"

When you and I grew up, authors, journalists, people who wrote white papers and reporters were thought leaders. They shared their ideas and research through standard news channels or via association peer review processes.

The definition today is much broader.

A thought leader can be someone who is sharing information through Twitter, LinkedIn, Facebook and other social media channels. This information can be original or not. Social media has given people an opportunity to create their own networks of people that are following them and a mouth piece to share their passions.

If your passion is early childhood education you can use your online community and social media channels to share:

- Interesting blog articles

- Retweets of information relevant that was shared with you

- A news article you read that you felt was excellent

- Youtube videos

Very quickly your network of supporters who probably would NOT have known about your interests and knowledge in this area will quickly become aware of them and viola; you are the "thought leader" in this area! The more you are recognized by others, the more your reputation spreads and grows.

Remember just one person sharing a link you shared on Facebook could reach his or her 130 friends and if one of those friends shared it with his or her 130 friends, you just reached another 130 people and so on. The people that liked what you shared will reach out and connect with you. When they do, you are well on the way to building a bigger network of people who connect with your knowledge.

By doing this, new opportunities, friendships and business relationships develop.

We've talked previously about your student creating his or her own Twitter account and Blog and starting to find a voice. Your student should consider finding a niche in his or her areas of interest and passions and start sharing information across channels and writing blog articles. This will work for marketing, health, sports, engineering, speech, and literally any major. We have predicted that in the next few years, companies will be hiring students who have already started to build their thought leadership because they know if their organization is to thrive, it will need to have people that can get its message out there.

I shared an example with you earlier of how my daughter's blogging led to an opportunity for an expense-paid trip from Whole Foods to Costa Rica to blog about the company's sustainability program. Just recently, she blogged and shared photos of a tiny house concept that has a loyal, but small following. The creator of the tiny house, linked to her blog and delivered 1,000 visitors in one day.

It's all about thought leadership and getting in the game.

April was amazed, and of course is jazzed to see that the process is starting to work for her. It takes time, work and --instead of watching TV or hanging out-- your student will need to be researching and writing. April went through 3 other blogs before she landed on her "Sustainability Small" blog and a passion for living within the means our earth can support. Her voice is growing daily.

So your challenge to your student will be for him or her to find a voice, find a passion, and reach out to others with similar interests—then, to stay at it!

SUMMARY

So there you have it --12 guerilla marketing techniques to help your graduate get interviews and get the job of his or her dreams. We're not saying your student has to do all 12. Share these with your student to see which ones he or she feels comfortable with and start with those. I guarantee your student will find something that will light him or her up!

COMING UP

Business leaders since the day I began looking for a job decades ago pouted and complained that the graduates weren't ready for prime time. We're going to share 15 common complaints and concerns leaders are sharing about graduates today, and offer suggestions and advice on how your grad can use this knowledge.

A graduation ceremony is an event where the commencement speaker tells thousands of students dressed in identical caps and gowns that 'individuality' is the key to success.

- Robert Orben, Comedian

YOUR TO DO'S AND NOTES!

_____

_____

_____

_____

_____

_____

_____

_____

_____

CHAPTER RESOURCES

| *Visit Your College Career Center!* | **Free Video on Guerilla Marketing Techniques** www.theunemployedgrad.com | We've assembled 20 unique, fun, yet proven techniques that will help your grad get the CAREER job they want! Free! |

9

15 "SOFT SKILLS" BUSINESS LEADERS EXPECT!

Your student's college will not teach him or her the "soft skills" business leaders have been complaining graduates have lacked for decades. Start coaching your grad and improve his or her "soft skills" to help him or her stand out from others and launch a successful career.

Hard skills are traditionally viewed by employers to be those related to your student's degree. Hard skills come from the curriculum, lectures, research and training students get from colleges that are required for them to graduate.

Soft skills are not picked up in classes, but will be critical to his or her success in business. Don't get me wrong, a diploma is going to be very important in helping your student land a first job, but I think you will be surprised to learn that research shows that only 15% of one's success is determined by hard skills, while the remaining 85% of one's success depends on soft skills.

Soft skills relate to personal qualities, habits, attitudes, interests and social graces that taken as a whole make a successful employee.

Soft skills include things like:

- Writing skills

- Presentation skills

- Teamwork skills

- Interpersonal (gets along well with others) skills

- A good work ethic

- Time management

- Multitasking skills

- Ability to meet deadlines

- Professionalism

- Knowledge of business etiquette

A number of surveys by corporate hiring managers ranked communication skills, which include speaking, listening and writing, as being the most valuable and desired soft skills by department managers.

Business leaders are looking for candidates that can:

- Manage their time--where they can plan, delegate, schedule, prioritize, set goals, create and manage to-do lists and more!

- Communicate the corporate position to customers, share departmental policy or research within company or partner meetings.

- Stand up in front of a group or organization and professionally represent the firm.

- Create well written letters, documents and reports that are distributed through client and customer channels.

- Listen before they talk!

Soft skills are very important to companies because the world of work is built on people working together to get things done. They have to learn how to communicate with different personality types, to overcome personal hang-ups and do their jobs. It is critical for your student to be able to have great listening skills and behaviors in order to hear what others are saying so he or she can successfully complete projects.

If you make sure your student is taking ownership of developing soft skills and demonstrates them during the job search process, he or she will not only get more job offers, but will be well on his or her way to future leadership roles.

BUSINESSES DON'T THINK YOUR GRADUATE IS READY FOR THE CORPORATE WORLD

The Accrediting Council for Independent Colleges and Schools, the nation's largest accrediting organization of degree-granting institutions, engaged FTI Consulting to conduct a survey of hiring decision-makers in order to learn how college grad job applicants are perceived with regards to the knowledge and skills they need to succeed in the workplace.

The results published in November 2011, showed the industry thinks higher education could be doing a better job preparing graduates for the workplace. According to the research:

- Only 7% believe the higher education system does an "excellent" job preparing students, while 54% say it does a "good" job and 39% say "only fair" or "poor."

- 45% of decision-makers believe that most students would be better served by an education that specifically prepares them for the workplace. 55% prefer a broad-based education that helps them choose a best career path.

- Hiring decision-makers admit to difficulties in finding the right applicants to fill open positions.

- Only 16% say that applicants are "very prepared" with the knowledge and skills they would need for the job. 63% say applicants are "somewhat prepared" and another 21% say applicants are "unprepared."

- 54% of hiring decision-makers report that the process of finding applicants with the necessary skills and knowledge set is difficult.

- 29% of decision-makers say that finding the right applicant has become more difficult over the past few years. Only 15% say it has become easier.

I've not seen a report in a long time that is saying as strongly as this report suggests that business professionals are looking for improvements in the "product" they are being offered. This study is not saying students don't have a foundation and understanding of the curriculum they took, they are just saying that students don't have the "soft skills" they need.

SOFT SKILLS ARE NOT TAUGHT IN COLLEGE

Students are coming out of a campus environment that is much more relaxed and stepping into a corporate environment about which they have no clue what the rules, regulations and culture are all about.

Hiring managers and business professionals complain graduating seniors DON'T:

- Understand the importance of arriving to work on time

- Stand up to greet a customer or be introduced to a superior

- Communicate effectively

- Show respect for coworkers and managers

- Work well within teams

- Complete assignments on time

- Dress appropriately

- Put in a full 8 hours of work

- Look for more work when they complete projects

- Maintain a clean work area

- Focus on the job and spend too much time on social media and texting

You could help your student "shine" brighter than any other applicants by encouraging them to master qualities and traits business professionals are looking for.

The following is a list compiled from numerous surveys of hiring managers and business leaders of attributes they believe students are lacking.

1. Good communication skills

2. Interpersonal skills

3. Creative problem solver

4. Working within a team

5. Integrity and ethics

6. Self confidence

7. Motivated and committed

8. Leadership skills

9. Quick adaptability to change and uncertainty

10. Good listening skills

11. Commitment to lifetime learning

12. Commitment to excellence

13. Willingness to take risks

14. Willingness to face assessment

15. Commitment to turn in reports

Elaine Barrett, Director of Ethical Skills and Training, a United Kingdom company, sums up the importance of your student acquiring soft skills.

> "Despite businesses putting as much emphasis on 'soft skills' as the technical competences to do the job, employers as well as the wider education system have not yet woken up to the fact that they need to invest the time and resources into helping these young employees develop the way in which they communicate, interact with others and present themselves. Unless this attitude changes, young people will be increasingly alienated within the job market."

Because colleges and universities are not teaching your student soft skills and businesses don't want to take the time, it will be up to your student to take ownership of this and take the time to improve his or her soft skills.

Let's take a look at each of these to see what business leaders are looking for and see if we can kick around some ideas about how you can encourage your student to pick up experience and skills in these areas.

Your student does not have to master all of these, but if he or she is going to be a productive contributor to an organization's mission and goals, eventually he or she will need to be well grounded in as many as possible.

1) Good communication skills

This is probably the most common complaint businesses and organizational leaders have about recent graduates. Unless your student is graduating with an education degree, or law degree, they probably did not get enough exposure in communicating thoughts or positions through formal presentations in class and briefs and reports.

Businesses and organizations are looking for people that can not only speak well, but put their thoughts on paper. They need people they can put in front of their clients that will impress the clients, not embarrass them. This doesn't mean your student needs to be a great orator, but they do need to be able to analyze situations, and communicate a position in a professional manner backed by logic and facts, not emotions.

A good way to help your student get exposure to this is to make sure your student:

- Takes speech classes

- Joins the college debate team

- Joins the local Toastmasters

- Holds leadership positions within campus organizations

Some people are naturals at this, but most of us need some help in overcoming our inhabitations, particularly speaking in front of groups of people, small or large. As studies show up to 75% of us are afraid to speak in front of a group of people, chances are, your student will welcome some help in this area.

Your student has a number of resources available to him or her including books, tapes and even a search on YouTube that will deliver sources he or she can go to for advice.

2) Interpersonal skills

Ninety nine percent of all businesses in America are small businesses with fewer than 16 people working in them. The people that run these companies are entrepreneurs, children of founders, or those who started in entry level positions.

Typically in small businesses, managers have to wear a lot of hats and accept a job description that always adds more, but rarely takes anything off!

As a result, few small business leaders get formal training in running a business and managing people. They are so busy running their businesses that they can't work on their business and people issues.

Have you watched the hit TV show, The Office?

On a weekly basis, Michael, the manager of Dunder Mifflin, the company featured in the TV show, shocks his staff by making decisions that pit employee against employee, showing favoritism and setting the wrong example. While this boss is not the mean kind, he is definitely dysfunctional, sometimes loveable, and many times despised.

Mid-sized and larger companies face similar situations although they often have budgets and plans to handle interpersonal relationships, sexual harassment, how to deal with difficult people, etc.

So your student would be better prepared if he or she spends some time participating in clubs or volunteered in community organizations to gain a better understanding prior to graduating about how to deal with people. Your student should also do some investigation and reading on his or her own.

Your student is going to have to learn how to:

- Deal with difficult colleagues and superiors

- Listen to co-workers

- Compromise

- Share successes and failures

- Report to colleagues and a boss!

It takes time to learn and manage these skills but once accomplished, they will help your graduate quickly advance within the organizations. It's best to learn these skills early in one's career!

A video tape I fell in love with about 20 years ago and one that is still relevant today is Richard Flint's, *A Day at the Zoo* (now on CD). Richard compares 18 different animals to the types of personalities grads will find in offices. It's a fun way for people who have never stepped into an office to learn how to judge personality types, learn how to deal with them, and communicate with them.

Office politics and people can destroy creativity and ruin careers. The one gift you can give your grad is a solid understanding of how to work with others successfully.

3) Creative problem solver

Before the turn of the 20th century (makes me sound old), my firm did a great deal of business/education partnering.

We partnered with a local high school and used our (at the time) new technology called voicemail, to develop asynchronous coaching relationships with students. Because it was difficult to get to the school to mentor students, we decided to see if we could use technology to let both the mentor and mentee communicate whenever it was convenient for them. So when my student wanted to ask a question, he or she called and left a message. When I wanted to share something with the student, I'd call and leave a message.

One of the things that became apparent to me while working with high school teachers is that the rote method of memorization was not as important to my company as creativity. I didn't need someone who could remember Civil War battles, I needed people that could solve problems and work with customers.

My point, way back in 1980, was that computers would become a more dependable source of information for facts that our brains did not have to store. What we needed were people that could look at a problem, evaluate the available information, and develop creative solutions. I encouraged the teachers to add curriculum to support the development of creative skills.

In many conversations over the years, I've argued that the leaders of companies in the future will not be those that have the highest IQ's, tested well, or had the best grades. They will be individuals who will know how to sift through data and reach out to their peers to find creative, ongoing improvements in their products and services.

Now some 30 years later, the Internet has given everyone an opportunity to become a "good enough" expert in just about anything. Using the internet, within four hours, I can source out data, experts, best practices and write a report on nearly anything. I used that technique to write this book in just 30 days. The Internet also enables me to source out names, events and examples to spice up this book. I could not have written this book without the internet and the collective wisdom of the billions of people that add to its knowledge base.

You will need to encourage your student to learn how to use the enormous amount of data, information and contacts that are available through the web, via blogs, videos, magazines, newspapers and social media to solve problems.

They will need to know how to:

- Pose questions and solicit advice from other professionals on LinkedIn, Facebook or even Twitter who are dealing with the same issues.

- Use crowd sourcing to gain advice and input from the public at large to test out theories, new products and/or emerging ideas for their companies.

- Use Social Media to field test their research and/or reports so they can further refine it.

- Hire people from around the world at 1/20th the cost to conduct research or implement strategies

So that is your challenge and your goal. You need to open your student's eyes to what he or she is facing and ask your student what he or she added to a job today that a computer couldn't do tomorrow.

- Factory and union members didn't ask that question a decade ago and now find robots doing jobs for which they once earned over $30 per hour. These robots work 24/7, never take vacations, never have health or personality issues and they run on oil and electricity!

- Secretaries and receptionists didn't ask that question when automated phone systems and answering machines as well as word processing software were introduced which literally decimated their jobs.

- The 20,000 member travel agent industry did not have time to react when the Internet made it possible and preferable for people to set up their own flights and hotels and book their own cars.

Today's worker needs to be in a constant state of personal development and building his or her knowledge credentials, or that worker risks being replaced initially by low cost foreign workers who are every bit as competent, or eventually by computers, SmartPhones or SmartPads.

At the height of his career Thomas Edison set a personal goal to create a minor invention every 10 weeks and a major invention every 6 months. It's no wonder he spent most of the time at his lab. The man was not only driven, but he was a creative genius.

While we all can't be as driven as Thomas Edison, his goal setting and creativity provides an example we can all aspire to! Creativity starts with asking questions and the questions your student should start asking should focus on uncovering pains and problems that need to be solved within a business.

We've shared a number of those, but you might encourage your student to pick up any number of books that are designed to spark creativity. One that I can think of off the top of my head is *Cracking Creativity, The Secrets of Creative Genius* by Michael Michalko. Michael provides exercises, techniques and proven strategies to get even those with limited opinions thinking out of the box!

4) Work within a team

Learning how to work well in teams is so important, not only in business, but also in families. As parents, we help businesses and our kids' careers by giving them chores, and keeping them accountable and responsible.

We are entering an era where companies are recognizing their organizations can become much more effective if they pull the right people together and use their collective and individual skills for short or even long term projects. John Foster, Head of Talent and Organization for Hulu wrote in his blog,

> "Teams solve difficult problems better than individuals. We believe in small teams and big ideas, and that familiarity breeds innovation. Our teams are not just a format for working together; they are the best way to manage the ambiguity and uncertainty inherent in our business."

Teams also help organizations explore new opportunities faster with more firepower. As companies begin to understand how to better inventory skill sets both in and outside their boundaries, they will be able to quickly ramp up a team with minimal effort. Working in teams will become ever more virtual as companies and employees increase their use of social media, online web meetings, and collaborative software.

I'm a big fan of Salesforce, a SaaS CRM software program that enables me to store my contacts, sent template emails and letters and keep a history of all activity. The software is constantly being improved and the latest innovation is providing a Facebook like news feed where members of a group or team can see the "chatter" and activity that is happening around an event, activity, prospect project, or client.

It's a great tool to keep team members informed of what is being accomplished, who is handling issues, and for them to provide input on the fly. This helps:

- Reduce redundancy

- Speed up processes

- Keep everyone in the loop

- Reduce the need for meetings

All of that spells more revenue and less cost!

Being a team member will require your student to adopt and use new technology successfully.

Other traits your student will need to have in order to work successfully include the abilities to:

- Work collaboratively with others

- Follow through on commitments

- Meet deadlines

- Provide recognition and acknowledgement of others' contributions

- Push others when they are falling behind

- Be able to organize and juggle responsibilities

Again, not all of these skills are taught or learned in schools, but they are all a very important part of being a productive member of an organization.

If your student is interested in picking up some tips on how to work with groups, the above suggestions will get them started. One book I've enjoyed over the years that will help them understand how to work with others in meetings is *Death by Meetings* by Patrick Lencioni. Group meetings cost time and money and frequently, participants fail to take notes, fail to follow up and in the end, and decisions made in meetings take months if not years to complete.

If your graduate knows how to conduct themselves in meetings, and how to run meetings, I promise you they will get not only get noticed by upper management, but they will find themselves moving up the ranks quickly.

5) Integrity and ethics

Companies are built on the culture, and the core values of the people that support it. We live in an era where companies are buying into social responsibilities, sustainability strategies, employee and company volunteering, and community responsibility, yet, in the past decade we've seen powerful companies disintegrate overnight because of the lack of Integrity and ethics of their staffs.

Anderson Consulting and Enron are just two examples of organizations whose quest for profits "sold out" their ethics which resulted in their companies imploding.

Social media and the viral effects it provides can take a good company's reputation and almost destroy it over night. It doesn't have to be a CEO or upper management who does the damage. Consider these low level employees that gave their firms black eyes.

An employee of Ketchum Advertising made unflattering remarks on his Twitter account ("I'd die if I had to live here,") about Memphis,

Tennessee, the headquarters of FedEx. Unfortunately, he made the tweet on the morning he and his team were presenting a digital media proposal to the worldwide communications group at FedEx.

One of FedEx's staff members picked up the Tweet and forwarded to everyone up the food chain in FedEx, as well as at Ketchum. You might say a storm of criticism fell on the employee that tweeted that message. The employee received a rather direct response from a company spokesperson that said,

> "Many of my peers and I feel this is inappropriate. We do not know the total millions of dollars FedEx Corporation pays Ketchum annually for the valuable and important work your company does for us around the globe. We are confident, however, it is enough to expect a greater level of respect and awareness from someone in your position as a vice president at a major global player in your industry."

Ouch! I wonder if they kept the account or where the employee works today? Note that social media made it possible for the entire world to see management's response to his tweet!

In another, more recent, situation over the Christmas holiday, nearly everyone at first gasped, and then chuckled, when a home security camera caught a FedEx employee literally throwing a large screen TV over a fence and into a yard of a customer. Not only was the TV bruised, but so was FedEx's reputation.

This is a perfect example of how one employee can ruin the reputation of a company with tens of thousands of employees. How many consumers do you think decided to go to UPS to ship their packages after seeing that video clip?

Ouch again!

Here's just one more example of how a single employee can put a company in hot water in an online and connected world.

Comcast, one of the largest cable companies in the nation, had their reputation set back by one of their repairmen. As the story goes, the repairman was at a customer's home and needed some input from his company. He used the customer's phone and called his support team only to be put on hold for nearly an hour! As he sat on the customer's couch, he fell asleep! The homeowner videotaped the Comcast repairman asleep on his couch and posted it to YouTube.

Almost overnight, the late night talk show hosts, water cooler discussions, and family dinner discussions focused on the poor customer service that was endemic within utilities like cable companies. The video has been viewed by tens of millions of people on YouTube and is still brought up from time to time, now 4 years later.

The good news, however, is that examples like these are improving customer service departments around the globe. No successful company can give lip service to customers. They really have to care!

These are just a few of the incredibly embarrassing situations companies have to deal with that are not caused by upper management, but by the rank and file staff. Your students will need to understand that companies are looking harder at the integrity and ethics and even financial acumen of prospective employees.

It's very common for companies to do a complete background check on employees. Nationwide Company in Columbus, Ohio, uses third party companies to check on the accuracy of resumes. They closely check for actual start and stop dates, reasons for leaving the company and confirm pay information. If any of this is out of step from what the prospective employee has said either in writing or verbally, it could knock him or her out of competition, because the company is questioning integrity.

Companies like Nationwide use standard credit checking services to add one more element to their decision process. In a day and age when there are 4-6 people vying for every job, companies can be very particular on who they hire and, the good companies are doing their due diligence so they not only get the best, but they can also increase employee retention.

Your graduate needs to know a few simple things to prove his or her ethics:

- Arrive on time and leave at the agreed upon end of work day.

- Acknowledge others for their participation on projects, reports and activities.

- Be honest in everything he or she does.

Doing so will mean an easier climb up the corporate ladder.

6) Self confidence

Wikipedia defines self confidence as:

> The socio-psychological concept of **self-confidence** relates to self-assuredness in one's personal judgment, ability, power, etc., sometimes manifested excessively. Being confident in yourself is infectious and if you present yourself well, others will want to follow in your foot steps towards success.

My definition of self-confidence was when I saw Bruce Springsteen in our college gym with a very small audience in the early 1970's. My friends and I were blown away by Springsteen's sense of confidence on stage. He owned it. Nearly 40 years later; he still steps on stage and delivers more energy, passion and life than most of us could muster in a week!

That's the kind of confidence we want your graduate to have when he or she heads out in the business world.

For most companies, employee confidence is one of its greatest resources. It's the most difficult skill to develop in people. Companies are no different than great sports teams or bands. When the right players come together there is nothing the team or band can't achieve. A business does not survive on one leader, but its success is dependent on the team that makes up that company.

That's why companies take so long to hire. Besides being afraid they are going to make a wrong decision, they want to keep looking for that person who has the confidence and spirit that will help the company grow.

Is your student confident?

- Some say confidence is a gift and part of one's DNA
- Others say confidence is earned, not learned.

I'm guessing you'd agree with me that anyone can become more confident as long as he or she has had the right training, time to adapt, and has been able to witness how it's done!

Confidence comes from coaches, experts, and yes - even you.

You've been giving your child confidence for his or her entire life by recognizing him or her for achievements, acknowledging things he or she did that were above and beyond. Now that your student is entering the real world, he or she needs to be able to walk into a first job with a good understanding of what the corporate world is expecting of him or her.

There are a number of ways you can help your graduate build self confidence. Consider any one of these.

- Remind your grad they have accomplished something that less than 30% of the population has achieved – a college degree.

- Remind your grad of the activities, awards, recognition and accomplishments he or she has.

Encourage your grad to:

- Dress for success.

- Compliment others.

- Be willing to compromise but make sure his or her position is known.

- Know what his or her fears are and have a plan to work on them.

- Over prepare for presentations and meetings.

- Admit when he or she is wrong.

- Admit when he or she doesn't know.

Confidence gets easier with experience, knowledge and preparation. There are bazillions of books, tapes and professionals out there that can help your student become more confident.

Basic human behavior doesn't change.

A good book to read is one written by a fellow Ohio resident, Norman Vincent Peale. Peale's, book *The Power of Positive Thinking* was published in 1952 and has sold 20 million copies.

Peale himself confessed that as a child he had the worst inferiority complex of anyone. His book came out of his personal desire to grow past his fears and become all that he could be. It worked for him. Besides becoming an ordained pastor after attending Ohio Wesleyan University, he also wrote over 40 books, founded the Guidepost Magazine, and hosted a weekly radio program for 54 years. From a shy, introverted childhood, Norman grew beyond his fears and continues today to influence millions of people today.

It all starts with your grad. He or she will need to find that spark, that intuition, passion or desire to accomplish or do something of value for themselves or others.

7) Leadership skills

Few people are born leaders, but many people can be trained to be leaders. Shy people, introverts, all kinds of people have learned to, under the right circumstances, reach beyond their insecurities to step into leadership positions.

If you want your student to succeed, he or she will need to step into leadership positions on sports teams and in clubs and organizations as early in life as possible. He or she will need to understand the role of a leader, how to lead, and how to be led.

Many of the traits we've been discussing are mandatory for leaders, but let's do an audit of a few more to see what your student will need to assume leadership positions.

1. Confidence

2. Empathetic but firm

3. Thought leader within his/her area of business

4. Decisive

5. Knowledgeable on how to build a team

6. Consensus builder

Let's take a look at each of these and see which of these areas your student will need help in.

Confidence

A leader has to embrace the company vision, mission and goals and build confidence in the staff that he or she can help make those come true. We're not talking about being a braggart, but being able to inspire everyone in the organization, yet show respect and care for the people, customers and mission.

Empathetic but firm

A leader can only lead if he or she has earned the respect of those they lead.

A good leader has to also be a good listener and be able to see issues from others' perspectives, and at times even step into their shoes to gain more insight. Leaders are not buddies during business hours, they are the stewards of the mission and their sole purpose is to keep everyone on track in the company's, department's, and individual's goals. That means there are times when leaders have to take a firm stance and push individuals and teams to higher levels of performance.

Thought leader within his/her area of business

The internet is flattening the organization and giving everyone access to people and information.

A junior level staff person's personal blog can spew out insightful ideas and strategies, and gain a wider audience then someone in the executive suite. Everyone in an organization today has an opportunity to share thought leadership and written strategies through social media channels.

However, when your student does this, he or she needs to share facts, best practices, and discuss current situations from a position of knowledge and research. This requires leaders to absorb a great deal of industry information during non business hours just to stay ahead of the flood of others moving in the same direction.

Decisive

As I write this, we are at the beginning of a political campaign where candidates are accusing each other of flip-flopping on issues and not standing for specific ideals.

To most, every issue has a twist that --depending on the audience-- requires a different solution. Your student will not only need to gather the knowledge he or she needs to make decisions but will need to be able to stand behind those decisions and do everything they can to make them a reality.

Knowledgeable on how to build a team

An effective leader is like a coach. He or she knows how to put teams together, motivate them and get them working efficiently. He or she needs to be able to assess talents, skills and build excitement and confidence in the team's challenges. The leader needs to know how to get out of the way and at the same time build in accountability.

Consensus builder

Successful leaders have to know how to get people to work together and to push them to do extraordinary things. Along the way leaders also need to learn how to compromise and build a final strategy that incorporates the best ideas. A leader needs to know how to promote and nurture this environment and how to make it safe for people to share ideas.

If your student has held a position within a club or organization on campus, he or she just took baby steps in learning how to lead and be led. You should encourage your student to continue to develop leadership skills – before and after they leave campus.

John Maxwell has written more business books then I can count, but one that you may want your graduate to read is his *The 21 Irrefutable Laws of Leadership: Follow Them and People Will Follow You.*

8) Motivated and committed

The millennial generation has been characterized as one that has benefited (or not - depending on the point of view) from the continual input, or help of their parents (some referred to as, "helicopter parents").

True to the term, helicopter parents hover over their children and gently nudge them, coddle them, and encourage them. Some characterize the millennial generation as one that waits for others to do things and make things happen.

Certainly this is a broad generalization and I'm sure there are varying degrees to which parents are more involved in their kids' lives than in previous generations. I recently read an article that indicated some hiring managers were seeing more parents showing up with their kids for interviews! Not a good thing!

Companies and organizations are looking for people who show up to work who are motivated to fulfill the responsibilities on their job descriptions. Business leaders are far too busy to have to baby sit employees and encourage them to do an assignment or task or hold a conversation sharing with them the big picture about why those employees need to get it done.

Managers want what they need, when they need it.

They are also looking for high levels of commitment. Work doesn't always stop at 5:00 p.m., nor does it start at 8:15, 23 or 45. Managers need a support crew that is loyal and can fulfill personal and company commitments – every time!

To prove their motivation and commitment your graduate will need to show:

- A real commitment to their work and assignments

- Ability to deliver their work on when needed, without being reminded

- An entrepreneurial spirit and interest in improving the company

It sounds easy but these characteristics do not come naturally for everyone!

9) Quick adaptability to change and uncertainty

Spencer Johnson and Kenneth Blanchard wrote an easy to read book called, *Who Moved My Cheese,* that outlined the effects change has on people. It offered advice on how people who are change-averse can learn to accept change and go with the flow.

The premise of the book is something culture and society has been dealing with for centuries. Heraclitus of Ephesus, a Greek philosopher (c.535 BC - 475 BC), is one of the first people credited with saying, "The only constant is change." His quote, which seemed to be relevant to his times, is even more relevant to ours.

In a recent report by IBM called the Global Catalyst that surveyed CEO's of some of the top companies in the world, the leaders all expressed one of their biggest challenges will be to drive their companies through a cycle of nearly continuous change and uncertainty.

The report also supports my personal belief that companies today and in the future need creative people. They need people who know how to use thousands of inputs from people, computers, reports and industry buzz-- who can create the products to solve the problems the company faces.

Here are additional challenges CEO's said they faced as they were building global companies:

- Cultivating creative leaders—those can more nimbly lead in complex, global environments

- Mobilizing for greater speed and flexibility—producing significantly greater capability to adjust underlying costs and faster ways to allocate talent

- Capitalizing on collective intelligence—through much more effective collaboration across increasingly global teams

If major corporations see change and the ramifications of this within their firms, your student will need to be equipped with the right frame of mind, skills and knowledge about how he or she can help those companies live in a continuous state of change.

If he or she is recognized early in a career – your grad has a bright future ahead.

10) Good listening skills

A small percentage of the population fall into the category of, "natural listeners. "

Good listeners are the people you feel you can tell anything to. My wife is like that. She'll meet someone at a Starbucks, the isle of the grocery store, or at the post office, and before Gae knows it, the people she meets will be confiding things they probably haven't shared with their therapists. She not only knows how to listen, but she knows the right questions to let the person release more information that seems natural and not like prying. I've always told her she missed a career in law enforcement!

Listening skills are mandatory for anyone involved in the corporate life, from boardroom, to sales, customer service, product development and manufacturing, everyone needs to be in tune with each other or risk making costly mistakes.

Poor listening can result in bosses misunderstanding what is said, departments snubbing each other over misunderstandings or customers feeling miffed because the firm did not hear them.

Dr. Mark Goulston, author of *Just Listen: Discover the Secret to Get Through to Anyone*, shares his thoughts:

> "Most people upshift when they want to get through to other people. They persuade. They encourage. They argue. They push. And in the process, they create resistance. When you use the techniques I've proven to work, you'll do exactly the opposite – you'll listen, ask, mirror, and reflect back to people what you've heard. When you do, they will feel seen, understood, and felt- and that unexpected downshift will draw them to you".

Ask your student if they received any training or skill building in listening while in college. Chances are your student did not.

When your graduate steps into the corporation, he or she will be anxious to show off knowledge. If he or she does so too soon, without gaining an understanding of what was asked, he or she could give others the wrong first impression.

Companies are complex entities. They are ruled by a culture defined by people, hierarchy and policies. <u>Your graduate will need to be cognizant of this and use his or her ears more than mouth in the first month!</u>

11) Commitment to lifetime learning

It seems kind of ironic that students make a commitment of time, money and effort in obtaining a four year degree and then stop learning.

I guess you might say – life gets in the way!

Unless it is required of their profession, like a doctor, lawyer or someone in the financial investment industry, a vast majority of college graduates hang up their curiosity and interest in learning new things.

As a culture we spend a tremendous amount of time learning baseball or golf standings or statistics of personal players, or watching the lives unfold and blow up of those on shows like the *Bachelor, Famous Housewives of* (fill in the blank), or the antics of a group of millennials from New Jersey.

Hopefully you will be able to instill an interest or thirst in your student to continue his or her studies and education after graduation. Today your grad has access to both online and convenient evening and weekend programs for post graduate degrees, and at the same time has access to some of the world's greatest minds on nearly any topic through free online education programs such as the MIT Open Courseware program.

There are 2,000 plus courses offered and many by the same professors that students are paying thousands of dollars per course hour to take. The courses provide video lectures and MIT has made a commitment to continue to upgrade the delivery mechanism to make courses more interesting and easier for students anywhere in the world to take.

Companies will be looking for your student to participate in programs offered by:

- Industry associations

- Local community colleges (related to their work)

- Online advanced degrees

- Local programs like Toastmasters

Things are changing so rapidly today, thankfully the Internet did come along or we wouldn't hear about these things for years. It should be relatively easy for your student to continue to pick up knowledge and training in today's web based learning environment.

12) Commitment to excellence

Like the examples we shared of employees who gave their companies black eyes, companies today are facing stiff global competition, and need to continuously improve their products, reduce costs or offer more for the same amount.

In today's company, a commitment to excellence cannot be a phrase the marketing staff emblazons on the videos, flyers and other marketing paraphernalia, but it must be something that every employee inculcates into the culture. Every person in the company needs to have a commitment to the company adhering to excellence.

Your student needs to step into the company culture with a strong understanding about why he or she needs to deliver the very best, no matter what job your student has been assigned, and he or she needs to do it every time.

Your grad needs to understand that it only takes one disappointed customer to start an avalanche of complaints and/or discussions through social media channels.

We shared stories earlier in the book about employees from Comcast, FedEx and other companies whose performance gave their companies a black eye. Every employee has his or her own personal responsibility to perform at the highest level. One of the top managers in a previous company I founded had a theory that struck me at the time as odd but the more I thought about it, the more I realized he was right on. John's theory was that a company is only as strong as the weakest employee. In his opinion if a company doesn't correct the behaviors and performance of the weakest employee, every employee will "dumb down" to the level of the weak employee.

To help your student gain a better understanding about how excellent companies perform, I might recommend he or she read, *In Search of Excellence: Lessons from America's Best-Run Companies*, by Tom Peters and Robert Waterman.

13) Willingness to take risks

During the dot com boom in the late 90's one of the most often repeated phrases by entrepreneurs and business leaders was "Ready – Fire – Aim."

The point was in the rapidly changing--or should I say *booming*-- dot com time, it was more important to MOVE, or to start something and worry about the overall strategy and plan later. There was so much excitement about the new opportunities the internet was providing. Nearly every field was wide open with little or no competition. This made the "first mover" advantage important to startups. The goal was to quickly increase membership/participation and secure a position in the market.

A lot of that attitude and entrepreneurial spirit is again in demand in companies today. Entrepreneurial skills and attitudes include:

- Actively looking for a problem and writing down solutions

- Building consensus within the company of the change that is necessary

- Continually looking for ways to cut costs

- Reaching out to other departments and customers to find new products to develop

Your graduate is going to need to be seen not as a cog, but a solutions provider, a go to person that is continually looking for solutions and building on a culture of continual improvement for the company.

Your graduate has to understand that the successful companies of the future will be driven from the bottom up!

To support an environment we've discussed that is continually changing with brutal downward pressure on costs, companies can no longer play it safe.

14) Willingness to face assessment

The job review time is one of those high stress moments that employees dread.

The vast majority of job reviews are done poorly. They either are too subjective and are not based a good job description that defines outcomes and goals correctly or they are conducted using computerized tools that drop in paragraphs on topics that are pretty meaningless. However, they *are* important.

We suggest your student makes sure he or she has a clear understanding of the job description and what he or she is supposed to do. If the job description does not spell out how he or she will be considered successful in any of the responsibilities, your grad needs to ask the boss what he or she expects to be accomplished within each area of responsibility.

Based on that, your student can easily provide management with a review of what he or she has accomplished in each area.

15) Commitment to reports

I've employed hundreds of people in my career and have found most people avoid providing reports in a timely manner because they don't want to be accountable. If you can't impress anything else on your student, this is the big one.

<u>Your student needs to find out what his or her management expects reported upon, weekly, monthly, and quarterly and to be the first to hand in those reports</u>. Ideally, your grad could go one step further and provide analysis of ups, downs, and issues faced that might have prevented him or her from accomplishing something and --above all-- offer ideas and solutions to the problems he or she sees manifesting in his or her department that will affect his or her ability to do the job in the near future.

I suggest your student have a conversation with the boss to make sure he/she understands exactly what the boss is looking for. Make sure your grad gets into details to understand:

- What the report needs to include

- How it should be formatted

- If it should be in a spreadsheet or a word document

- If it should be emailed or dropped on a desk

- When it should be delivered

Your grad needs to understand that his or her job is to be like the canary in the mine. He or she is closer to the daily activities in his or her department then his or her bosses. If your grad is not reporting issues on paper with recommendations to resolve those issues, they are not helping management to solve them.

Too often management is running in 18 different directions and a conversation that is half heard is not heard at all.

Your student has to understand his or her responsibilities to their colleagues and boss. These need to be written down and discussed later at length.

SUMMARY

Your students have a lot of work to catch up in these soft skills. This is not a problem that started with the millennial generation. Employers have been complaining that college graduates for years are a bit "green" and do not have these skills. It's a global situation.

Grads are about to enter the professional workforce with more knowledge and information packed into their little brains than any graduates prior to them. However, they, like generations of graduates, will lack in the soft skills and knowledge that business professionals have been asking colleges to provide in graduates for decades.

This is not part of the college curriculum so unless you encourage your student to take some time and invest in his or her soft skills, he or she won't have them by the time he or she starts looking for a job.

It doesn't take a rocket scientist to learn these; your grad just needs to be made aware. When they are, I guarantee he or she will stand heads above others.

COMING UP

The job search process is very complicated. It's easy to forget something or overlook what seemed to be a small thing and then later learn that small thing-- in our mind something inconsequential -- prevented us from getting a job. We'll now look at common mistakes your grad can avoid!

Obstacles are those frightful things you see when you take your eyes off your goal.

- Henry Ford, Industrialist

YOUR TO DO'S AND NOTES!

_____

_____

_____

_____

_____

_____

_____

_____

_____

_____

CHAPTER RESOURCES

10

18 MISTAKES YOUR STUDENT WILL MAKE

*W*eve had access to the top hiring managers in the nation to learn the common mistakes graduates make. Now you can coach your graduate to avoid these so they get the job!

Looking for a job is a time consuming, gut retching, and for most people, an emotional rollercoaster.

Nearly every college graduate is entering uncharted waters when he or she starts a professional job search. The only experience one usually has comes from applying for part time and summer jobs, which pretty much only required them to show up and look responsible.

Many people get stuck in the process for far too long because they just don't have a clue about how to plan for, search for, and execute the job search. As a result they make lots of mistakes along the way.

We don't want that to happen to your graduate!

So let's look at the common mistakes that hiring managers say your graduate will make. You can take this information and begin to coach your student to avoid making these mistakes.

The eighteen most common mistakes graduates make are:

1. Not visiting the career center

2. Not exploring career options

3. Failure to build a career plan

4. Failure to develop a job search strategy

5. Spending too little time on the job search

6. Not employing multiple job search techniques

7. Not getting an inside contact to deliver resumes

8. Not controlling the job search process

9. Focusing too much on job boards

10. Looking only for job openings

11. Letting rejection become overwhelming

12. Not including industry keywords in their resume

13. Waiting for the hiring managers to call

14. Not providing specific details of accomplishments

15. Lack of preparation for interviews

16. Not developing a professional network

17. Failing to clean up social media sites

18. Not developing a personal brand

It's a bit overwhelming isn't it?

Not to worry-- Let's take some time to look at these issues individually and give you some details about how you can work with your student prevent any one of these issues from preventing your student from getting the job of his or her dreams.

1) Not visiting the career center

In chapter 7 we identified our number one - most important strategy - that your student should adopt is visit the college career center. Nearly all that we are familiar with have assessments that your student can take to get to better know what career path they should be exploring.

Your student, if like most, will probably not step into the career center until their senior year, and --even if they do-- they'll visit only a couple times.

Why is that?

The career center does not have any authority over students. They can't require students to explore career opportunities, to attend meetings, or even build a career plan and job search strategy. Only a handful of colleges have a program in place that requires students to invest time and create a written career plan.

While working with career centers, I started to realize how under staffed and funded they were, and I wrote a white paper that offered 10 ways they could get more resources from upper management. But, after sharing this with over 300 career centers, I finally understood that even if they got more funding to add career courses and tools that would make the career center available 24/7, students would not take advantage of those resources.

Surveys support this.

The National Association of Colleges and Employers conducts yearly studies to benchmark the industry so they can see trends and their members can implement strategies to provide better services to their customers.

One of their surveys measures the average visits to the career centers by graduating seniors. According to the survey:

- 27.2% never visited the career center.

- 16.1% visited once.

- 18.2% visited twice.

- 27.0% visited 4-6 times.

- 11.6% visited 8 times.

This is hardly enough to even get help on their resumes!

Yet, additional surveys show that --after graduation-- grads wish they had visited the career center and done more to prepare for their careers. A survey conducted by Adecco showed that 71 percent of recent college graduates wished they had done something differently to prepare for the job market.

Additionally the survey found:

- 26% wished they had started their job search earlier – while in college.

- 26% wished they had spent more time networking.

- 26% wished they had applied for more jobs.

- 43% were currently working at a job that did not require a college degree.

Despite the fact that career centers are understaffed and funded, I can guarantee you that the staff will do everything in their power to help your student *if he or she asks for it*!

If he or she does visit the career center and take ownership of a career plan, your student will be in a better position to have a job by graduation. Assuming this, your student can be earning $3,000 to $4,000 a month more than grads who did not take their job searches seriously. With the average grad taking over 7 months to find a job after graduation, that could be $21,000 to $28,000 more in your student's pocket.

2) Not exploring career opportunities

The most important thing your student should do in his or her freshman year is to take a series of assessments to get to know where his or her personality and skills will flourish. Unfortunately based on the stats we just reviewed, most students skip this step, even though it's personally and professionally fun and rewarding!

Many millennials will spend more time evaluating which smart phone to purchase then evaluating career opportunities.

We recommend they take the following assessments:

- Personality/Behavior

- Interest

- Skills

- Branding

Then, sit down with a professional that can interpret the results and provide them feedback. The career center is a good place to start to take these assessments, or your student can gain the counsel and advice of career coaches who carry an assortment of these and are certified in interpreting them for your student.

With that knowledge your student should start to explore the types of careers, positions, industries and companies that best suit his or her skills. As he or she starts to narrow down what interests, he or she should start following blogs, sign up for industry newsletters and connect with alumni who are in these fields to begin to get a more in-depth understanding of the industry.

To further a comprehension of the industry, a student should try to job shadow alumni contacts either in person or virtually with a goal of getting one of them to offer an internship.

So many people skip this step and start thinking about it after they graduate, only to discover they choose the wrong major and are heading into the wrong career path.

It's costly to skip this step. Those that do not invest in exploring career opportunities:

- Change majors while in college and as a result have to go a 5th, sometimes a sixth year

- Have a greater likelihood to be in the 50% of students that start college but never will finish, or the 60% that take 6 years to complete their degree

- Be among the 17 million people who are working in jobs that do not require a college degree!

The bottom line is that it's costly to skip this step. If your student is not jazzed about a major, if he or she is not getting input from others on how to apply what he or she is learning in a career, there is a greater chance your student will fall within the stats we just reviewed.

If your student is near graduation or at graduation, it's never too late to take assessments and explore careers opportunities. Better now than 10 years from now.

For more details on what your student should be doing to explore career opportunities refer back to chapter 7.

3) Failure to develop a job search strategy

I'm a big proponent of spending time developing a job search strategy. A job search strategy is simply their plan that details:

- What your student will do each day

- What job search techniques your student will use

- Who your student will call, who your student will email, and with whom your student will network

It includes not only actions, but *goals*.

Successful job searches start with developing a daily routine and knowing what to do next. If your student is "winging it" and trying a few different things each day, he or she will get disappointed, dejected and likely take a few days off because, "It's not worth doing anything."

Without a daily plan, your graduate will run out of things to do, and hit a brick wall, get distracted, and quit for the day. The next day he or she will start again, and this time your student will get through what he or she knows to do quicker, and then quit for the day. The third day, he or she will procrastinate and take a day off thinking that he or she can get done what needs to be done the next day -- and so it goes.

A plan, and I mean a daily plan, written out by the hour, will keep your student focused and on track. It's really the key to a successful job search. By staying true to a plan and keeping consistent, results will come. Tony Beshara, author of the *Job Search Strategy* considers it a numbers game. He has meticulously tracked the success of the 8,000 people he has put into positions. He reminds his clients:

- It will take 100 calls to reach 10 hiring managers of which 2 will have jobs available.

- It will take on average 16 interviews to get a job.

- Most students and first time job seekers drop out of this process by the 20th phone call and 8th interview.

It's a numbers game and your student has to understand that.

A good book to pick up tips and ideas on how to launch a successful job search strategy is Tony Beshara's, *The Job Search Solution.* Tony outlines specific steps, time commitment and techniques based the proven results of his clients.

4) Failure to create a career plan

The career plan is their lifelong blue print of:

- What he or she wants to do

- Where he or she wants to go

- For whom he or she wants to work

- What he or she wants to earn

We want your student to look into the future to see what he or she wants to be doing 3, 6, 9 and 20 years from now. Without a written career plan, he or she will bump from job to job without potentially building on his or her previous knowledge and successes.

His or her career plan is a blue print he or she will refer back to and modify his or her entire working career.

Assessments, job search strategies, and a personal career profile are part of the career plan. With the knowledge your student has about himself or herself and his or her skills, he or she needs to be thinking about the:

- Level of responsibilities and titles desired 3, 5 and 10 years into a career

- Earning ranges desired in 3, 5, and 10 years into a career

- Triggers, events, and issues that will cause your student to move on to the next position

Think of a career plan as a business plan. It's a plan that will outline where he or she wants to take his or her "business"! Just like a business plan, your graduate will need to have core components of it.

We recommend at minimum it includes a:

- Career Plan Summary

- Career Plan Vision & Mission

- Career Goals

- Career Market Analysis

- Career Path

- Networking Strategy

- Career Plan Conclusion

Research shows that writing down goals and strategies increase the likelihood those goals and strategies will happen. A study of Harvard MBAs in 1979 showed that:

- 84 percent had no specific goals.

- 13 percent had goals that were not committed to paper.

- 3 percent had clear written goals and plans to accomplish those goals.

Then in 1989 the same group was interviewed:

- The 13 percent of the class who had goals were earning, on average, twice as much as the 84 percent who had no goals.

- The 3 percent of the class who had clear, written goals, were earning, on average, 10 ten times as much as the other 97 percent put together!

Share this with your student. Your student can either choose a life that will see him or her fall in with the 97 percent, or by investing just a little bit of time, achieve more then her or she ever dreamed of!

5) Spending too little time on his or her job search

We featured Richard Bolles, author of the book, *What Color is Your Parachute* that has sold over 10,000,000 copies in our TalentMarks Grad Career Webinar series.

Richard has influenced more careers and career professionals than any career expert on the planet. During his presentation he shared that research was showing graduates spend about an hour a week on their job searches. I was pretty shocked and had to ask him to repeat it just in case I might not have heard him correctly.

Later that year, in the summer after the students had graduated, TalentMarks sponsored and produced a 12-hour online Career Marathon featuring 24 career authors and experts. During the transitions from speaker to speaker we conducted a series of polls. One of the questions was, "How much time do you invest in your job search?" Over 60% of the students indicated 1-5 hours per week.

Wow, that pretty much confirmed what Richard Bolles said.

In my opinion this is not because graduates are lazy, they just don't know better. They have no clue as to how much time and effort one has to put into his or her job search.

It's not just graduates!

According to Donald Asher, author of *The Hidden Job Market*, the average adult job seeker invests only 6 hours a week on his or her job search!

Looking for a job is a full time job

With 80 percent of students unemployed on graduation day, virtually all of them are destined to a long, protracted job search that will cost them thousands of dollars in lost salaries and probably delay their chances of starting their adult lives because they have to move home during this process.

Your student has to understand that looking for a job is a full time job. That means the student is working at it for a minimum of 8 hours per day. Joyce Russell, EVP and President of Adecco Staff US agrees:

> "Regardless of how the economy is fairing, graduates who proactively pound the pavement well before they finish their studies are more successful in landing a full-time job after graduation. The best piece of advice for the graduating class of 2011 is to treat their job searches as if they are full-time jobs. The students who succeed are those who proactively put themselves out there and build relationships by networking with professors, working closely with university career centers, actively connecting with alumni, and capitalizing on real-world job experiences through internships and temporary work."

It's like anything else. You student will get out of his or her job search what he or she puts into it. I can guarantee you that if he or she is investing more time in his or her job search, he or she will have more opportunities presented in the long run.

Peter Weddle is a well know career expert that has written a book called, Work Strong, Your Personal Career Fitness System. Peter looks at developing a job search strategy and plan as something that you have to work at every day. The way Peter looks at it, if someone is committed to work out to keep their body health, they need to have a plan to work on that will keep their career healthy. It's a good read that when taken to heart, will help build powerful new behaviors that will advance your grads career.

6) Not employing multiple job search techniques

Today, job seekers really have more channels and opportunities to look for jobs. When I started my career-- and probably when you did, too-- the only way to look for jobs was through the classified ads.

Today, your student should be using any and all of these channels:

- LinkedIn will help your student build a professional network across industries and build exposure.

- Facebook will help your student connect with recent grads who are working that can introduce your student to management at their companies.

- Twitter will enable your student to see jobs nearly as they are posted and get a first-mover opportunity to apply to those jobs. It will also enable students to connect to upper management and follow their tweets.

- Reading niche blogs that list jobs within the industry or hosting his or her own blog to show his or her "thought leadership".

- Making direct phone calls to companies who were recently awarded new contracts or reported a record year.

There are two additional resources we highly suggest your student adopt:

- Career Coach
- Job Search Buddies

If you can't be a coach to your graduate, hire one!

A career coach can cut months off the job search process by helping the graduate keep focused on his or her job search plans to help keep him or her on track. A coach can help the grad through the emotional ups and downs, and be an excellent sounding board that shifts through the emotions and keeps your grad on an even keel, building sound logical strategies and next steps.

I highly suggest you consider engaging a career coach in the critical months after graduation as he or she can help support your investment and also provide input to you on what you, the student, and the coach can do to make your student's job search strategy a success.

Job Search Buddies are the people you surround yourself with to bitch, moan, and complain about the last rejection letter, the screwed up interview and/or lack of responses from hiring managers. They are kindred spirits that are going through the same pains and walking down the same paths. We create Job Search Buddy groups that enable grads to blow off steam but to also offer encouragement and mentoring to each other. It's not an AA kind of thing, but close.

We encourage students and/or graduates to meet weekly using existing social media tools, like Google Hangouts or conference calls. In order to be a Job Search Buddy, a job seeker has to agree to the 12 responsibilities they have with their group members. It's the cheapest and most effective way to keep your student's attitude and commitment to his or her job search on track.

Among your student's responsibilities are that he or she reports to the others what he or she has accomplished in his or her job search that week. Remember, we are all about numbers and these meetings are not all about the emotional thing, but having peers that keep you on track.

7) Not getting an inside contact to deliver resumes

I've read a lot of inside industry news in doing research for this book and I was surprised how frequently I heard hiring managers, career coaches and even students say, "Sending unsolicited resumes is a pretty worthless process."

If your student is sending resumes without an inside contact, - even if it makes it past those digital keyword searches, it will get less than a 30 second glance by the hiring managers– even though a graduate might have labored on it for months!

Don't believe me?

- Starbucks received 7.6 MILLION job applicants over 12 months for about 65,000 corporate and retail job openings.

- Procter & Gamble received nearly 2 MILLION applications in 12 months for 2,000 new positions, and for vacant jobs.

- Texas Roadhouse, the retail restaurant chain with 350 locations around the nation receives on average 400 resumes for a job opening within 24 hours of it being listed online!

- Google received 2 MILLION applications for the 7,000 positions they filled in 2011.

You might be better at math than I, but what do you think the odds are that your student's resume would get noticed if it was included in these HUGE pools of applicants?

We've recommended your student find people who work within companies first and connect and engage with them PRIOR to sending in a resume. It takes companies a good 6 months to fill a position, so a student has plenty of time to build a relationship before he or she shares a resume.

How does one do that?

First a student should search within the company for an alum that works there. It doesn't matter what year in the alum graduated. If a student can't find an alum, have your student look for someone with similar interests, geographical background, high school, or other similarities that offer a chance for your student to connect with that alum. Once they locate the inside person, your student needs to reach out and let that person know that he or she is a student, that he or she reviewed the person's profile, and thought the insider would be a great person to connect with from time to time as he or she advances in his or her career.

If the insider denies the request or ignores it, your student is going to have to move on to a second choice. He or she could make multiple requests of people in the same company but caution your student to make sure these insiders are from different departments. Then, once a student has established a relationship, your student can periodically ask questions about the company, issues, what it's like to work there, and then-- perhaps 3 weeks into the relationship-- approach the person to let him or her know a job came to your student's attention that they are interested in, and ask if he or she would they be willing to drop your student's resume to the hiring manager personally.

There are two other ways students can find "inside" people. One is the Facebook application Branchout and another is Monster's version call Reachout. Both give your student an unbelievable opportunity to develop relationships that would have been literally impossible prior to these tools.

8) Not controlling the job search process

Typically, without a plan, job-seekers react, not act.

By that, I mean they react like Pavlov's dogs to stimuli they can relate to. For example, students will see a job posted that looks relevant, so they send a resume. However they don't write down to whom it was sent, the recipient's contact information, or a time to follow up.

Worse, the job might not be in the direction your student outlined in his or her career plan, but because he or she feels the need to do something, he or she will apply anywhere.

We suggest every action have subsequent actions that are carefully timed and delivered in order to consistently take advantage of the time and effort your student invests.

For example, as part of your student's job search plan, he or she should not send out a resume unless they have a follow up plan like this one:

1) Send an email 3-5 days later with a link to his or her online blog that will provide decision makers with a chance of seeing his or her "thought leadership" skills.

2) Immediately after sending the resume contact the "inside person" to let this person know a resume was sent (assuming her or she was not able to get the person to hand deliver it to the hiring manager).

3) Follow up 7 days after the email with a video email where he or she talks about an article regarding the company and/or industry and if possible, show what he or she has done in his or her college career when faced with similar issues.

4) About 7 days later after interviewing the "inside person," write a letter to the hiring manager indicating an understanding that the company is involved in (fill in the blank) initiatives and offer evidence about how he/she can be an asset.

5) When following the company's Twitter, Facebook and/or LinkedIn accounts, continue to share thoughts and ideas which will keep his or her face in front of staff and contacts.

6) Perhaps a week letter, I'd suggest you take a copy of the job description provided and help your student create a power point presentation that highlights the requirements page per page and visuals-- examples of reports, portfolios, work and past employment or leadership positions that give your student the knowledge to accomplish the job.

<u>Remember your student has had ZILCH training on how to search for a job and the common response is to let the process control him or her, not vice versa.</u> They will naturally sit back and wait for the employers to take the next step, which is fundamentally, diametrically opposite of what they need to do.

Your graduate will need to learn how to develop this game plan so they can control the job search process. When your student controls the job search process, and implements a diversified communication strategy he or she will impress the heck out of hiring managers.

Why?

Hiring managers today are looking for creative, persistent and professional people. The skills we are sharing are the same skills they employ on a daily basis to fulfill their job openings.

9) Focusing too much Job boards

It's not unusual for inexperienced job seekers to spend most of their time on job boards. For most, it's a matter of ignorance. They don't know there are a dozen other channels they could be looking into. As a result, what they don't know is hurting their chances to get jobs.

They really need is to have a dozen job search techniques.

Why?

 We've seen reports that suggest that the average job seeker will spend 40 hours a month on job boards, searching, applying, and updating information.   Yet, stats are showing less than 12 percent of jobs that are offered (keep in mind I said offered, not accepted) are made as a result of the connections happening on job boards.

Two very successful job search techniques include applying right through the company website and via networking.   Research by CareerXroads confirms that.   Their research shows that within major corporations:

- 30% of jobs are filled through referrals.

- 22% are filled through the corporate web site.

Let's assume that the average person was spending 3 hours a day or 60 hours a month on his or her job search.   Assuming that the average person spent 40 hours per month on job boards, that would represent nearly 70% of his or her job search time.

Some of the more popular job boards include, Indeed, Monster, CareerBuilder, AfterCollege, HotJobs, CraigsList and the literally thousands (some estimate 50,000) of niche job boards that associations, blogs, companies and others develop. We advise students to pick 2-3 primary sites to keep in touch with and another 2-3 they check on periodically. It takes a bit of skill and knowledge to understand not only which are the best job boards, but how to use them. Many job boards are now incorporating social media tools that will enable your student to find out which of his or her friends are working at the companies they are interested in so they can use the "insider connection" strategy we've talked about.

Job boards are one of the easiest job search techniques and because they don't require human contact, or immediate rejection, many people end up spending the most time on them.   Steven Rothberg, President of College Recruiter, warns graduates that if they are going to use job boards they need to have a strategy to follow up on jobs they apply for:

> "People have this mistaken impression that the job board they're using is magic. They apply to 200 jobs and then sit back and wait for the phone to ring."

Job boards are not just for locating the right jobs applying, but they can also be used to gathering information about companies and the jobs themselves.

Better companies will create profiles that will provide information like:

- Company atmosphere
- Products, services and employees
- Benefits of working at the company (including paying for school tuition, child care, maternity/paternity leave, paying for physical activities, etc.)
- Opportunities that give to employees resources for personal and professional growth and development

Research is showing people look for jobs using the following techniques:

- Google
- Company Webpage
- Company CareerSite
- Google (company research)
- Social Media
- Job Board
- Friends
- Company Job Posting

There is an art and science to using job boards and we encourage your student to learn more about the best practices prior to starting. Some suggestions we've collected from hiring managers, recruiters and job seekers include:

- Use a powerful headline for your resume

- Don't make your identifying information confidential

Dan Schawbel author of the book *Me 2.0* is more blunt on his advice regarding job boards:

"A study by Jobs2web, Inc. shows that companies look through about 219 applications per job through a major job board before finding someone to hire. They only look at 33 applications per hire on their own corporate career site! Just as I said in my book *Me 2.0*, job boards are black holes. Stop submitting your resume to them and praying that a machine finds it and delivers it to a hiring manager. You should spend more time meeting people at companies where you want to work."

We're not saying not to use job boards, but use them as a part of the overall strategy.

10) Looking only for job openings

I recently read that 40 percent of jobs that are filled happen as a result of a company finding a great prospect and then creating a position for that person. The stat sounds kind of high to me, but it does open a discussion about the importance of your student networking with people and organizations from the perspective of a consultant.

What do I mean by that?

Simply that while your student is talking to his or her network, and family and friends, he or she needs to not only ask if these people are aware of jobs that may be available, or to keep eyes out for positions, but they should be asking about their companies and how those companies are doing.

In fact, I'd prefer if your student spends most of his or her time learning about the company, the issues they are facing, and problems they have not been able to solve. They should be prepared with a series of questions. Once they have these down, they are easy to remember. In fact it, being able to discuss them will become automatic. Here are some examples:

- So John, How are things going at your company?

- Has the recession affected your revenue and product development?

- What are you doing differently now to generate new revenue?

- How is that going for your organization?

- What do you think is your company's greatest challenge today?

- What would your management say the company's greatest challenge is today?

- Are there any new projects being proposed or worked on?

- How can I learn more about this issue so I might propose some options to your management?

Then, they can find out who they need to approach.

Your student could then approach those key people and suggest working on a short term assignment to evaluate the problem, talking with the departments involved, and producing a report with suggestions.

The company would have --for a very small investment-- someone that would have the time to begin to take a look at the situation and then use his or her suggestions to formulate recommendations for them to take advantage of. If management perceives this as a viable process, your student just created a new position for himself or herself.

You may think your student doesn't have the experience or savvy business skills to step into this kind of role, but I would disagree. Colleges today require students to participate in group projects that require brainstorming, teamwork and analytics. They've had to take positions and solve problems.

This is just another way for your student to use skills he or she picked up in college.

11) Letting rejection become overwhelming

Let's face it, job hunting sucks!

The typical job hunter is out there on his or her own, trying to land a job that will enable him or her to support a family and hopefully fund a retirement account along the way. They don't have office buddies to talk to, they've got bills to pay, and they are stressed-- and worried!

- Nothing about it is easy.

- It makes everyone anxious.

- It can be darn right scary!

I like to remind job seekers they have it easy compared to salespeople, actors and actresses. These people go into "job interviews" multiple times a day! They have to do their bests to show off their products/talents in order to get their jobs or orders.

For an actor/actress it's particularly brutal. First of all, he or she is not being paid to go to audition, and he or she probably had to assemble a specific wardrobe for an audition, and then practice the script, drive an hour to the audition, wait an hour for a turn, walk in, do a two-minute read and then drive the hour home. In actors' worlds, like sales peoples' worlds, the product may be the wrong size, color, an older model, etc.

Rejection gets you closer to yes!

The one thing we know in almost any job search is that a rejection just means you are getting closer to a YES. So we have to keep your student focused on remembering this is a numbers game and that each rejection is a step in the right direction.

There are a couple of things your student should always do with rejections.

1. Call, email or write a thank you note to the hiring manager and thank him or her for his or her time. It's always a good idea to find out what he or she would have needed to get the job. If it's a job they really, really want, it doesn't hurt to contact the hiring manager 3-6 months later and check in. You never know, sometimes the candidates don't work out and end up getting fired!

2. The other thing is to find out the name of the person who the company is hiring and what company that person currently works for. Why? Think about it for a second... The person that just got hired has to resign from a job, which means his or her former company will be looking for someone. If

you happen to call that company within a week of the other applicant getting hired, you have a first-mover opportunity to solve that company's problem.

As a parent you can encourage your student during the job search process.

Remind your student:

- To not take it personally – competition is fierce

- That they are not alone -- 13 million others are in his or her shoes experiencing the same thing

- Keep it in perspective – your student might have been overqualified or faced a situation where someone else with less qualifications was recommended by an inside connection

- Accept reality – remember it will take 16 interviews to land a job, so this "no" just puts your student one step closer to an offer

The bottom line is, you can be an enormous help and be there to keep his or her confidence high!

Consider reading The Panic Free Job Search by Paul Hill. Hill provides ideas and solutions that will keep your grad moving forward and not becoming paralyzed because they don't know what to do next.

12) Not really knowing how to put together a professional resume

By now you are beginning to see how, at any point of the job search process, your student can get knocked out of the running.

If networking is low on your student's priority list, then a resume becomes a critical job search component. There are three primary mistakes made with resumes:

- Not enough of the right keywords are used.

- The wrong styles are used.

- The resume is not customized for the industry or position.

Keywords

In the old days (10 years ago!), a company would place an ad in the classifieds for a position and wait for resumes to be MAILED to the company. Some accepted phone calls. The time and effort for a job seeker to get his or her information to multiple jobs limited the number of resumes and candidates that would apply for a job.

Today, however, with the ease and no cost involved in submitting an electronic resume, candidates --qualified or not-- are submitting resumes for positions. This is putting an enormous amount of stress on hiring managers to sift through as many as 250 resumes to find the right candidates.

To help employers filter resumes, software has been developed that looks for keywords in an application that might indicate the candidate has the right stuff for a position. With a blink of an eye, the 250 resumes can be narrowed down to a manageable 25 or even less. That gives the hiring manager more time to review the candidates presented to him or her.

How does this work?

Programs will look at the keywords that define leadership, skills, knowledge and experience. It doesn't matter how pretty the resume looks, how many colors it has, or the scent added to grab the hiring manager's attention -- if it doesn't have the repeating keywords the organization defined for that position, it will end up in the digital "circular file"!

Programs will also look at experience.

As an example, PNC Financial Services uses an applicant tracking system for bank-teller positions. Its system is designed to look for specific experience, not just keywords. An applicant for a bank-teller job is automatically filtered out if his resume doesn't indicate that he has two to three years of cash handling experience.

Style

There are a dozen ways to build a resume. A resume style should be used to match the type of company a candidate is applying for. A technology company might accept a more informal style as its standard, a marketing company might prefer to see resumes adopting a more creative look, and a small business might prefer conventional resumes. That's not all. Resumes can be written for specific industries and careers that include professional, engineering, business, academic or even student specialties.

Resumes can also be organized in chronological order so they show how the candidate has progressed in his or her years, or can be more task-oriented to show the types of skills and experience the candidate has.

Customized

The third common mistake candidates make is sending the same resume for every position. The resume not only has to survive the electronic keyword filter, but it also has to grab the attention of the hiring manager. A hiring manager is going to spend more time on a resume that is organized and is sharing qualifications based on the skills and information the company requested.

In some cases it's best to lay out the resume, experience, etc. in the order the job description is organized. It makes it easier for the hiring manager.

A lot of people put an enormous amount of time into writing a resume. It's important to get it right, but they need to remember that it's only 1/20of the overall strategy.

In a Wall Street Journal article, Lauren Weber shared 5 tips from Josh Bersin, CEO of Bersin & Associates, and Rusty Rueff, career workplace expert at Glassdoor, on how your student can prevent his or her resume from falling into a "big black hole".

1. Forget about being creative. Instead, mimic the keywords in the job description as closely as possible. If you're applying to be a sales manager, make sure your résumé includes the words "sales" and "manage" (assuming you've done both)!

2. Visit the prospective employer's website to get a sense of the corporate culture. Do they use certain words to describe their values? If a firm has a professed interest in environmental sustainability, include relevant volunteer work or memberships

on your résumé. The company may have programmed related keywords into its resume screening software.

3. Keep the formatting on your résumé simple and streamlined—you don't want to perplex the software. With a past position, the system, "sometimes gets confused about which is the company, which is the position, and which are the dates you worked there," especially if they're all on a single line, says Mr. Bersin. To make sure you hit all the categories, put these items on separate lines, and,"Don't get cute with graphics and layout," says Mr. Rueff.

4. Some screening systems assign higher scores to elite schools. You may not have gotten your B.A. from a top-tier university, but if you attended a continuing education class at one, include such qualifications on your résumé.

5. Don't ever lie or exaggerate just to get through the screening process. Recruiters and ATS's are savvy about tricks jobseekers use (such as typing false qualifications in white font). "You don't want to get through the black hole and find out it's a worse hole you got yourself into," Mr. Rueff says.

Good tips from people who live and breathe this stuff everyday!

Martin Yate, has sold over 5,000,000 books in his *Knock em Dead* series. One of his books provides an up to date look at industry best practices and styles that will get your students resume notices. When you visit his website, look for his e-book on resumes that shares hundreds of resume templates.

13) Waiting for the hiring managers to call

You might remember on the cover of the book we had a grad laying down on the couch with his SmartPhone in his hand, waiting for a call he thinks he is going to get following an interview.

The one thing your student has to understand right now is that the hiring manager is not going to call your student when he or she said they would.

These are incredibly busy people who are continually on the phone, handling issues and crises within the company, and when he or she tells your student he or she will be getting back to your student in two weeks, tell your student not to count on it.

Quite frequently hiring gets stalled because:

- Someone involved in the process is not responding

- Of delays in background checks

- Of department issues or crises that crop up

It's going to be your student's responsibility to keep in touch with the hiring manager to keep his or her name in front of that manager.

We're not suggesting your student call every two weeks asking if the manager made a decision yet. What we'd prefer your student do is to create a drip marketing campaign that every 7-10 days drops information to the hiring manager about your student.

Your student needs to be proactive and activate a follow up "drip marketing" campaign as we discussed earlier to make sure the hiring manager keeps your student top of mind.

14) Not providing specific details of his or her accomplishments

Graduates have to keep in mind that hiring managers sit with prospective candidates all day, 40 hours a week, 160 hours a month, and analyze their responses, body language, and experience to see if the people they are interviewing are good fits for the positions and will add to the overall company culture.

Too often, when asked to explain what they did within a specific position, the interviewee will provide a detailed explanation of the tasks and issues they handled. One area he or she does not provide as much detail on is the stats, numbers and end results of his or her participation. Your student could stand out over others by sharing memorable stats that identify his or her productivity and contribution to the organization's bottom line.

For example, a student might be asked what his or her role was in a campus club or organization and respond that he or she was in charge of marketing the events and activities. To make an indelible impression on the hiring manager, he or she might expand an explanation to something like this:

> Prior to my taking the roll of marketing director for our club, our yearly event averaged 100 people. I decided to use a combination of marketing strategies to increase participation and revenue for the group on the same budget allocated the previous year.

> I diverted 20 percent of the marketing to Facebook ads and created a fan page for our group so we could drive more traffic through our members' networks of friends. I also had a group of members attend the football events each week holding up signs that drew attention to our event. The combination of increased exposure and use of viral marketing and advertising on Facebook doubled participation to 200!

Additionally your grad could show that he or she:

- Is a good communicator by his or her participation in the debate club OR, that he or she has joined a local Toastmasters Club

- Works well within a team by explaining participation in the Capstone project in college that required 6 people to design a marketing program for a real company

- Has good negotiating skills because he or she had two part time jobs in which he or she worked both in customer service and sales and in both cases had outstanding results

- Has had leadership experience with participation in clubs and organizations while on campus or in community volunteer areas

- Has passion for the industry by the fact that they belong to 8 LinkedIn industry groups with regular participation and the blog and tweets they share about that industry

The one impression your student has to leave the hiring manager with is that he or she understands that companies are driven by results. The best companies are run on a premise of continual improvement. They are always looking at the numbers to tweak and improve their systems and customer experience. Your student will stand out if they show they can fit into that culture without much training.

You need to help your student find these little nuggets in his or her short career to help your student be ready for those questions.

Eric Kramer has an interesting new way for job seekers to control the interview process and make sure the interviewer gets a clear picture of the interviewee's accomplishments. His book, *Active Interviewing* shows job seekers how to create a customized power point presentation that incorporates requirements of the position they are interviewing for, that includes proof of how they handle similar responsibilities in previous positions.

15) Lack of preparation for interviews

With so many people chasing the same jobs, it's quite an accomplishment to get an interview. It's so important to be prepared!

Your student should:

- Check the company's website to learn about the leadership and background.

- Review the past 3 months of press releases to gain an understanding of significant events within the company.

- Search Hoovers.com to learn who the company's competitors are.

- Follow up with his or her "inside connection" to gain additional insight.

- Ask for a job description ahead of time so he or she can be prepared to discuss how they have the qualifications and interests to accomplish the responsibilities required.

- Follow the company on LinkedIn to pick up "small talk" opportunities

Your student needs to find inside people who he or she can connect with. Have your student checked LinkedIn's search tool that allows your student to find alumni in the company and if he or she can't find an alum, use his or her network to find someone that could introduce your student to an insider at the company. If none of that works, your student should reach out directly to a couple of people prior to the interview.

Have your student check his or her Facebook friends to see if any of them are working at the firm too!

Your student needs to make sure he or she knows where the interview is. Some companies are huge and your student may think he or she allotted enough time to get there only to realize he or she has parked at the wrong building, and is then unable to locate parking at the right building and so end up being late for the interview. If this is the case, I guarantee your student will be disheveled and shaken up before he or she walks in the door!

16) Not developing a professional network

I think by now you are aware that nearly 80 percent of us get jobs through our professional network. Unfortunately, students leaving college have not developed a professional network and are essentially starting from scratch.

That's why we strongly suggest your student start introducing himself or herself to 5-10 alumni on LinkedIn each year. Students should develop a monthly dialogue with these contacts through social media, email and/or an occasional phone call.

Once a student is connected to alumni that are willing to mentor him or her, he or she should ask those people for two other introductions to those they think your student should meet. This will give your student a chance to grow his or her network at a faster rate.

Yours student can also use Facebook to network with the recent grads who are now finding their ways in companies and organizations around the world. It's not unusual for a graduate from college today to have over 500 or more friends which span multiple class years. So, make sure your student spends some time reviewing who he or she is connected with and reaches out to those connections.

Professional networking starts with a plan. Your student should:

- Have some idea of the type of person he or she wants to connect with.

- Know what he or she wants to learn from the mentor.

- Know how frequently he or she will connect and engage with a network contact.

- Know what value he or she can provide in a network.

A major mistake networkers make is not staying in touch with the network until they need something from a member of that network. It's a good idea to periodically send an email with a news article, blog link or information that might be relevant to the people in the network--or just an email or note card telling the network that the student is thinking of them and wishing them well.

Networking is not just an online experience, although this sort of networking will be easier for your student to master, but your student will need to gain experience in one on one and event networking, as well.

His or her college career center and alumni office probably holds networking events periodically and you should encourage your student to participate. These events will give your student some experience at meeting business people in an environment that is non-threatening and supportive. Not only will it help your student build his or her skills and feel more comfortable, but it will give your student more contacts to add to his or her database.

That leads to the final point I wanted to share about networking -- and this is a very common mistake people make. Very few people actually database their networks. They don't have the ability to pull out a list that has a network listed and/or any information that categorizes the members or provides data about what they can do to help the student.

There are a number of ways your student can do this. First and easiest is to get a spiral notebook and label it , "My Network." In the notebook, your student can simply start listing the people he or she considers to be a part of his or her network and include headings that gather email addresses, physical addresses, companies, industries and notes about the contacts. This same technique could be developed in a spreadsheet or word processing document. It just depends on which technique is the easiest for your student to use.

17) Failing to clean up social media sites

Jobs are won and lost as a result of information hiring managers find on social media sites.

According to research by CareerBuilder, 45% of employers use social media sites to screen prospective employees. That number is expected to grow. Of those who conduct online searches and background checks of job candidates:

- 29% use Facebook.

- 26% use LinkedIn.

- 21% use MySpace.

- 11% search blogs.

CareerBuilder's research showed the following primary situations resulted in people being thrown out of the "maybe" pile:

- Provocative or inappropriate photos or information

- Content showing a candidate drinking or using drugs

- Showing poor communication skills

- Making discriminatory comments

- Lying about his or her qualifications

- Sharing confidential or negative information about previous employer(s)

Graduates are leaving what they consider walled-in gardens where their actions and activities are shared on social media sites, particularly Facebook, Twitter and even YouTube. What they forget about this is how the photos, videos and statements they may have shared with others in the protected communities of their college friends could be looked at as negatives from hiring managers.

That's why it will be critically important for your student to go into his or her Facebook account and immediately put in filters and controls on what people can see. It's easy to do and will not affect the long term relationships with his or her friends. For example, on Facebook you have the ability to share information of any kind with everyone, friends, friends of friends, or in a granular fashion of only people in a specific list, only selected people, or only yourself.

There is no need to go back and delete all the photos out there of your student holding a beer can because he or she can go into his or her settings and set his or her controls so that information is only available to friends. Your student might consider racketing down who can see information during the job search phase and then consider opening it back up.

Positive effect

On the flip side your student's online community and social media participation can help your student. The CareerBuilder study we mentioned outlined the following areas that were viewed positively by hiring managers:

- Profile provided a good feel for the candidate's personality and fit.

- Profile supported candidate's professional qualifications.

- Candidate was creative.

- Candidate showed solid communication skills.

- Candidate was well-rounded.

- Other people posted good references about the candidate

- Candidate received awards and accolades.

This is just another example where your graduate has to be smart and be cognizant about how hiring managers think. Your student needs to put himself or herself into the hiring managers' shoes and make sure his or her online community and social media use is consistent with what the corporate world accepts.

<u>Remind your student they can control access.</u>

The reason your student needs to control access to his or her information is that a setting of "friends of friends" is quite broad. I may not want my parents to see my information but if I friend my uncle and my uncle is connected to my parents, as friends of my friend (my uncle), my parents have access to the things I didn't want them to see.

Your students can friend hiring managers and control what they see. For example they can put them under a list called, "Employers," and exclude that group from general posts they make, and/or include them in specific posts they want them to see.

So, make sure your student understands how this process works and the ramifications if he or she fails to make modifications.   You and I both would hate to see your student do everything right and then get knocked out of the running by failing to clean up and bolt down his or her online profile.

18) Not developing a personal brand

Finally, your student should spend some time evaluating his or her personal brand.

This involves reaching out to others to learn what they think of your student.   For example, your student may think of himself or herself as punctual, social, and a self starter.   Others may have a completely different vision based on his or her observation of the person.

William Arruda, a bestselling personal branding expert that speaks to corporations and their employees world-wide, has a unique and free way you can get started with a personal branding test.   Google "360-degree Reach" or William Arruda's name to check it out.

According to William,

> "360°Reach is the first and leading web-based personal brand assessment that helps you get the real story about how you are perceived by those around you. It gives you the critical feedback you need so you can expand your career

or business success. It's an integral part of the personal branding process and an indispensable tool for thriving in today's professional environment.

All your student has to do is register and fill in the email contacts he or she wants to, and these email contacts will provide their own opinions and insights. They will receive an email explaining what is being asked of them and told their comments will be confidential. The program will never divulge who said what.

The benefit your student will have is that he or she will be able to see general trends about what others think of him/her. As mentioned, this might be completely different than what a student thought of himself or herself. This is important because it will help your student take the things he or she wants to be identified for and continue to develop them, while creating a strategy for other areas where he or she is not recognized for.

SUMMARY

Who said it would be easy?

All it takes is just one mistake-- one oversight to blow an opportunity. Make sure your student is aware of these common mistakes and encourage your student to build strategies into his or her written job search plan to keep your student from making these mistakes.

COMING UP

Do you feel like you know a bit more than you did when you picked up this book? Your job now is to take this knowledge and do what you've done all your life-- be a resource and coach for your student. You've got the knowledge the information and you are now hip to the changes your student will face! Enjoy your new role!

Keep in mind that neither success nor failure is ever final.

- **Roger Babson**, College Founder

YOUR TO DO'S AND NOTES!

_____

_____

_____

_____

_____

_____

_____

_____

_____

_____

CHAPTER RESOURCES

Visit Your College Career Center!

News & Information
www.theunemployedgrad.com

Register for our eNewsletter and blog to get a steady diet of inspiring ideas, confidence building advice and strategies to get jobs! Free!

11

CAREER MANAGEMENT + HABIT + LUCK = CAREER SUCCESS

It's not just our colleges and universities that don't focus on career exploration, career planning and career management. Our society in general puts little focus on developing a systematic organized career planning and job search process that we can use for our entire lives.

There are too many other more entertaining ways to spend our time!

We live in a materialistic society that focuses a great deal of time and attention on products, services and the accumulation of things.

It's hard to escape becoming a consumer because each of us is inundated with advertising from the moments we begin to understand communication. Advertising started with a local bread maker putting a sign over his door. Later, mass printing techniques ushered in advertising in newspapers and magazines. Ben Franklin suggested starting a United States Postal Service which provided yet another way for merchants to sell their products. Then, merchants eventually got even newer channels to advertise known as radio and TV, which led us to something called the Internet only a couple of decades ago.

As a result of all of these advertising channels, it's impossible to escape the influence of merchants who are interested in changing our behaviors and solidifying our habits around their products and services.

Another area that influences our consuming habits is peer-to-peer influence, the type of influence we have over each other, as we all buy and consume products and services. "Keeping up with the Joneses" used to be a silent activity that played out when someone noticed a neighbor, friend or relative had something really cool that he or she wanted. Today, social media amplifies these desires a hundred fold as our neighbors, friends and acquaintances update their Facebook News Feeds and Tweet about the new things they are experiencing and doing. Every hour of every day, our friends' influences affect our behaviors and throughout the process, little by little, they also change our habits and our world.

Think for a moment what an alien might think of our culture when it first encountered us. The alien would see a:

- 10 billion dollar movie industry where people lined up to pay $8 to $12 each to watch the latest movie and spend billions of hours collectively watching a fantasy.

- 80 billion dollar online video gaming industry where people spend an inordinate amount of time playing games that engage them.

- 40 billion dollar sports sponsorship industry which has the sole goal of gaining the attention of consumers who spend endless hours tracking scores, reading articles, watching events, and talking endlessly at the water cooler and online about the last game, so that promoters can sell their products and services to them. The total annual revenue reportedly generated in the sports industry is a 414 billion dollars!

- 10 billion dollar beauty industry where we invest in everything from makeup, cologne and products that make us look younger, smell better and look fantastic!

- 20 billion dollar toy and hobby industry where people spend endless hours collecting and playing with things that add value to their lives.

- 100 billion dollar gambling industry that occupies the time and takes the money of everyone from the penny pitching elderly to oligarchs who might lose a million dollars a bet.

Each of these industries spends millions of dollars to encourage us to add their products and services to our daily activities.

Think about all the other ways we spend our time and money as consumers. The constant barrage of advertising influences our thoughts, desires and what we do in life. To be considered "normal" in our society, we pay attention and act on the messages merchants are sharing with us. These messages and the products and services they offer have created the culture in which we now live.

The consumptions that feed many of our interests are now being delivered through new electronic devices connected to the Internet almost –if not completely—on demand. In an astonishing few years, Apple has sold nearly 75 million iPads and nearly 200 million iPhones. These devices are changing our behaviors and habits in countless ways. As we continue to build our behaviors around these devices, every industry is clamoring to figure out how it can reach a customer base by using these new tools.

As a rite of passage for our children we will invest more money than the average third world citizen earns in a year in:

- Summer camps

- Bar Mitzvah/Bat Mitzvah celebrations

- Debutant Balls

- Vacations

- Sweet Sixteen parties

- Proms, Homecomings, Graduation parties

- Birthdays, Christmas and special anniversaries

I tend to think an alien would take a 30,000 foot view of our culture, activities and the time we commit to these activities and wonder why we spend so much time consuming products, services and celebrating events –rather than investing the time and effort it takes to develop our own creativities and our minds.

If you were lucky enough to be born into a democratic country like the United States, you've had the freedom to choose what you want to do with your life. What would our society be like if --instead of spending those billions in the industries listed above-- we spent more time and money mentoring and coaching not only our own kids, but those from other parts of our communities? What if our habits were different and we focused more on improving the lives of others, rather than consuming things?

What if we invested time each month in:

- Reading a self help, career book or career blog?

- Attending a presentation by a career expert?

- Engaging life/career coaches to help keep us developing productive behaviors?

- Investing our resources in programs that helped others start small businesses like Kiva and Kickstart?

- Talking around the water cooler about "cool" new products that are reducing our carbon footprint and raising the standards of living for people in third world countries?

- Tracking information and stats about career coaches whose students have gone on to accomplish new breakthroughs?

If we changed our behaviors and habits by doing more of the above, could we make a difference in the lives of our neighbors and global family?

While it might be a bit harder for us as adults to make these changes, it would be easier for our kids to adopt these new habits and make them an integral part of their lives.

It's never too late to switch gears and begin investing more time and thought into helping your son or daughter understand how to create a balance in their lives that includes commitment to the art and science of career management.

IT STARTS WITH CAREER MANAGEMENT

When your child made the decision to go to college, your son or daughter also took the first step toward change by exposing himself or herself to the information, experts and philosophies that can shape lives.

Your child's college experience will provide him or her with the tools, skills, knowledge and compassion to make the world a better place and help others who did not share the same luck, family and fortune to go to college. It will also give your child an opportunity, but not a guarantee, of a successful career and fulfilling life.

To gain the return on investment that you and your child want from his or her career, your child will have to focus on managing that career. We covered it in detail in chapter 4, but let's just review a few things as we wrap up.

You and I spent our younger years in a different time and era. We were able to stumble from one job to another with some degree of success and minimal unemployment.

Your student is facing dramatically different times and the old ways of "winging it" as a career strategy will not only *not* work, but will lead to a disastrous time of finding a career. Instead of being in control of one's career, those who don't adapt to the new realities of business and the job search process will struggle, become increasingly frustrated and find periods of unemployment increase as earning potentials decrease.

The changes we discussed in this book, including the techniques regarding how to look for a job, the introduction of social media, the competition from a globally highly educated, English speaking workforce, and computers that are bound to increasingly take over white color jobs all should represent a warning signal to you and your student.

The "lucky" few with jobs on graduation day will, of course, be those in high demand positions where there is competition for the candidates, but their company will also include people who thoughtfully:

- Explored career opportunities and created job search plans.

- Built their online presences and thought leadership skills.

- Created professional networks that focused on alumni and family friends.

- Studied the 15 "soft skills" companies are looking for.

- Did their best to not make the 18 common mistakes first time job hunters make.

Your student will need to take ownership of his or her career if not during the freshman year of college, as immediately as possible, even if it's on graduation day.

We've shown how high the stakes are. If your son or daughter does nothing there is a good chance your student will be among the:

1. 70-80 percent of the grads that will be unemployed on graduation day.

2. Grads that will take nearly 8 months to get a job.

3. 95% of students who will not have a written career plan.

4. 61% of grads who have had only 1 alumni mentor during college.

5. 60% of students that will spend less than 5 hours per week on a job search.

6. 60% of graduates working in jobs unrelated to their studies.

7. 58% of grads that wished they had worked more on developing their career plans while in college.

8. 80-85% of graduates that move home with their parents after college

The Associated Press issued a story that is being circulated just prior to the Class of 2012 graduating and suggests that 53 percent of recent college grads are jobless or underemployed. The story alludes to the fact that our college educated students are rapidly finding themselves in the same situation as grads in Greece and Spain where the economy is literally in shambles. Here is an excerpt from the story:

> About 1.5 million, or 53.6 percent, of bachelor's degree-holders under the age of 25 last year were jobless or underemployed, the highest share in at least 11 years. In 2000, the share was at a low of 41 percent, before the dot-com bust erased job gains for college graduates in the telecommunications and IT fields.
>
> Out of the 1.5 million who languished in the job market, about half were underemployed, an increase from the previous year.

Your son or daughter does not have to become part of these statistics if they he or she adopts the right career management behaviors today.

CAREER MANAGEMENT STARTS EARLY AND NEVER ENDS

When our kids were younger we involved them in youth sports, clubs and organizations like Boy Scouts, Girl Scouts and Brownies. We enrolled them in beauty pageants, spelling bees, events like the Soap Box Derby, and more.

Our goal was to help build their confidence, communication and interpersonal skills. These activities represented their first investments in developing their personalities, skills and knowledge that became the foundations they continued to build on.

You were there to coach your child through these first time experiences.

Can you think back to those times and what you dreamed your child would do when he or she grew up? In talking to hundreds of parents I've heard a variety of comments:

- "I just want (him or her) to be happy."

- "Johnny will step into the family business and eventually take it over."

- "Anne will become an engineer, (doctor, lawyer, dentist, etc.) like her father."

- "Ben will do great in business."

- "Andy has the people skills to excel in sales."

Whatever you dreamed, it is likely your dreams have influenced some of your child's decisions in picking a college, major and career. As Richard Bolles suggests, "it's highly likely your conversations about your job, the jobs of a colleagues, friends or relatives and or your opinion and the opinions of those around your child will keep him or her from moving toward a dream career."

Sometimes it's even what you don't say that can influence that decision.

My brother Ron is a perfect example of that!

Ron recently made a career change that resulted in him leaving a business he founded 18 years earlier so that he could enter the seminary to become a Lutheran minister.

He recently shared his story with me—it was the story of a career decision that took 30 years to make!

According to Ron, he was sitting on the bed of our cousin, Tim who had just graduated from Capital University in 1976, and Ron asked Tim what he was going to do. Tim shared with Ron that he was going to Trinity Seminary and planned to follow his father's calling to serve as a Lutheran minister. While I'm certain Tim doesn't remember the moment, for Ron, that moment was unforgettable. In a flash of an instant, Ron imagined himself as a pastor of a church.

A simple conversation between cousins sparked a thought that would haunt Ron for three decades.

Up until that point, Ron showed little interest in his classes at Lutheran West High School. He loved the theater, clubs and the spirit of the school, but dreaded tests, grades and writing reports. Ron graduated with about as low a grade point average as you can have to qualify for a diploma!

Assuming college was out of the question, Ron gravitated to a career that involved a lot of people contact.

In addition, he stayed active and involved in churches wherever he moved. People in the congregation frequently would tell him he'd make a terrific pastor. Ron would silently note it and, for a couple of reasons, bury the thought. To stay involved with churches and find "his" way to serve his community, Ron took a job with Lutheran Brotherhood Life Insurance Company (now Thrivent) and spent even more time in churches in and around his community.

Then, one day on the way home from church, his wife Esther broke into tears and asked him when he was going to answer his calling. At church that day, Esther had witnessed for the umpteenth time how natural Ron was in interacting with people, ministering to them and being a source of energy to them. Puzzled, Ron asked what she was talking about. "To become a minister," she told him -- Esther recognized where his passions were and knew he was not happy with the work he was doing. Ron tried to dismiss her comments by mentioning that he was involved in the church-- not only in leadership, worship but with the kids. In the back of his mind, he was thinking of all the reasons why he could not be a minister.

Then he made a comment to Esther that he had buried for a couple decades. He reminded her that when they first met many years and two kids ago, she asked him what he did for a living. "Don't you remember?" Ron said, "I replied that I was in sales" and then you came back and said, 'As long as you are not a pastor!' I've always assumed that you did not want to be a pastor's wife!"

Esther replied, "Ron, you have to remember what my relationship was with my mother then. If she suggested that my dream husband would be a doctor, I would have told you, 'As long as you are not a doctor!'"

Ron, still puzzled, drove on --thinking back to that moment when he had shoved the thought of becoming a pastor further back on the shelf and started questioning if he was doing what he was put on this earth to do.

Soon after Ron and Esther's discussion on the way home from church, Ron shared the conversation with our Mom. Mom mentioned that she and Dad frequently talked about how Ron would be a good pastor. Ron just about picked himself up off the floor in astonishment. He said to Mom, "You mean to say that you and Dad would have approved of me becoming a pastor?" She responded, "Of course Ron, we never said anything because we didn't think you were interested."

So there you have it.

Ron had an interest in the ministry, but he put it on a shelf because some of the most important people in his life innocently dismissed it as a possible career or never said anything about it to him. His future wife made an off the cuff comment that wasn't supposed to influence his decision, and Ron assumed from conversations around the house as he was growing up, that the ministry would be the last profession his Dad would want him to enter!

With the encouragement of his wife, Ron found the courage and strength to make the next decision. As he was nearing his 50's, he started to publicly announce his desire to become a Lutheran minister.

Changing careers as you approach 50 with two kids in college, a mortgage and no college degree, takes an enormous amount of guts and faith, particularly when you are heading toward a career that is noted to not include bonus plans and high salaries! Most people, including me, questioned the sanity of making such a dramatic move, but Ron had a lot of guts, passion and faith that he was finally making the right career decision!

In fact, that passion is why people gravitate to him and adore being around him. His infectious good humor and positive attitude lifts the spirits of everyone around him.

So Ron took the plunge and started the process to change careers. First, he had to take the necessary steps to qualify for seminary school and get his college degree. For the next two and on half years, he took courses, ran his business and continued to be a part of his church and family. It seems phenomenal that a guy that could barely pass a course in high school maintained such a wonderful academic record and graduated with honors and a 3.75 grade point average.

With degree in hand, he had to go through the rigorous process of applying for and entering seminary. At first, he was turned away, but that didn't stop him. He took what the admittance committee suggested that he do and completed the requirements. His second try resulted in an acceptance letter.

At the time I'm writing this, Ron is finishing up his first year in seminary. It continues to be an incredibly difficult challenge as he has to attend classes, volunteer at churches and hospitals, write reports and essays, and study, all the white, working a full time job.

However, if you talk to him today, he's on fire with excitement.

There is still a tremendous uncertainty in his future as there is with any college graduate. When he graduates, many people his age will be thinking about retiring, but Ron will have student loans to pay back, and there is no guarantee that he'll land in a church that can afford to pay enough for him to cover his living expenses and educational expenses.

Yet, Ron is lucky. He's acting on a dream job that he considered 3 decades ago, but had no idea how he could make happen.

Imagine if a career coach had been engaged with Ron while he was in high school. What if that career coach was able to help him work through the fears and concerns he had that prevented him from following his own intuition-- and committing to it. What if he communicated his interest and desire to become a pastor to his parents and his future wife? What if he had acted earlier on the constant encouragement and positive statements that the members of his congregation were making?

How many more people in his life would he had influenced, guided and consoled?

We need to make sure our kids have an opportunity to find and follow a path that will not only give them the most satisfaction, and personal and professional success, but one that will leave the world a better place for all of us.

You can't assume the college is providing your son or daughter with the tools, knowledge and resources they will need to get a job. We covered that at length in Chapter 2. We can't teach them the curriculum they need to qualify for their degrees, but as experienced job seekers who have the knowledge from this book, we can certainly guide, coach and be a resource in their first professional job searches.

The point in sharing Ron's story is to remind you the importance of you stepping in RIGHT now and take an active role in coaching and advising your son or daughter as they make the critical decisions that will determine the rest of their lives. To do that:

- Have heart to heart talks with them to find out who they admire, who they'd would most want to be like.

- Ask them what professions seem most interesting to them.

- Make sure they get exposed to people who are working in those industries by encouraging them to talk online, in person or email them. Require them to take notes and include this in their career exploration journal.

Ron's story is one of success, delayed.

It's a story of one human being fighting much harder then he would have had to, sacrificing more than most could endure, to change to a path his intuition and gut told him was right for him 30 years earlier.

While it has a happy ending, I'm sure you'd rather see your son or daughter have a better chance at making the right career decision when they start their career.

Your child may face this too, if he or she and you don't invest the time together today to carefully explore career options and expose them to career experiences that will "light their fire". Your job is not to just pay tuition. You more than anyone have a great deal at stake if you sit it out on the sidelines and assume they will "figure it out" on their own.

YOUR STUDENT NEEDS TO CREATE NEW HABITS AND BEHAVIORS

Your job is to help your student understand the significant risks of not investing 20-40 hours a year during college in career exploration, career planning and developing job search strategies.

Society, the culture of the college and peer pressure will be working against your child if he or she doesn't take ownership of his or her career the minute of arrival on campus or at least by graduation day!

While in college, students have to look at managing their careers as if it is a required course. That means changing habits and setting aside time if not each week, at least each month, to work on career exploration and their career plans. They don't have to be experts concerning all aspects of this; some will be natural networkers and find building their professional networks rewarding and fun. Others that are more strategic in their thoughts will dig building strategies around using social media and other online resources.

Richard Bolles, author of the best selling career book of all time, *What Color Is Your Parachute* agrees. He believes parents should take a more active role in introducing the concept of owning one's career and managing it as early as possible. To Richard, starting in elementary school is not too early!

Richard cautions parents about what they say about their own careers which can color their children's impressions of the business world. If a parent is struggling in his or her career and is constantly voicing issues while at home, the tone, repetition and intensity of the parent's comments will definitely color the child's perception of the work life. Bolles suggests that to offer advice and guidance to students, parents have to get right with their own careers, too.

According to Bolles, people job-hunt not the way the generation passes down to generations, but by the way those generations choose to live their lives.

He sees people living their lives in one of three ways:

1. Living their lives based on planning.

2. Living their lives based on intuition.

3. Living their lives based on luck.

Bolles believes the way each person chooses to go about his or her job-hunt is usually identical to the way he or she chooses to live life.

If Bolles is right, you have a pretty good idea right now which way your son or daughter is going to lead a career strategy. If your child tends to fall into the second or third category, this process will be a bit more of an adjustment for him or her. If he or she falls into the first category, your child will adopt to the concept of investing 20-40 hours a year in career planning with minimal adjustment to his or her habits and behaviors.

Most of us are driven by immediate satisfaction.

If we do something or invest in something, we want results right away. If we start a diet and skip a meal one day, we expect to see pounds drop off the next morning. If we are trying to learn a language, we get turned off because --after a month of effort-- we can barely introduce ourselves in that language.

Unfortunately, your student will have to understand that there is not an immediate pay off in the time and effort he or she will be investing in career exploration, career planning and job search strategies.

However, we can entice them and remind them of some immediate upsides to working on exploring careers and building career plans:

- They will get a chance to meet fascinating alumni working in career paths they are interested in.

- They will be able to find mentors and build new friendships with the career professionals they interact with.

- In relatively short time periods, these relationships can be leveraged into job shadowing and internship opportunities.

- Having a job immediately after graduation will enable them to purchase a car, take weekend trips and go to concerts and events.

WALKING ON THE RIGHT SIDE OF THE STREET

Our goal in writing this book was to make sure your student had the tools and skills so that he or she could have a shot at doing what he or she wants to do!

If your grad is creating a plan and focused on a strategy, there is a good chance that Lady Luck will knock on the door and help propel your child to the next level.

Luck plays an important part in all of our lives.

Your kids probably grew up on the scores of books and philosophy of Dr. Seuss. None of us would have been exposed to the *Cat in the Hat* had it not been for a chance run in on a street corner in New York.

The year was 1937 and Theodor Seuss Geisel was walking down a street in New York City, feeling totally dejected after 27 publishing houses rejected his book, *Mulberry Street.* He was broke, tired and rapidly losing confidence in his ability and dream of making a living as a writer of children's books.

As he was walking down the street, he bumped into a fellow Dartmouth alum and friend who happened to work at Vanguard Press, a division of Houghton Mifflin. His friend offered to take his manuscript and illustration to key decision-makers at the publishing house. The rest, as they say, is history. Vanguard Press gave him a chance and Theodor went on to publish 46 children's books that were converted to audio, movies and interactive games.

Like Rudolph Flesch, who introduced the Phonics method of reading, Theodor's mischievous cat wearing a tall red and white striped hat and a red bow tie offered an alternative, imaginative way for kids to learn how to read. His illustrations, rhymes and story lines encouraged children to explore their creativity and made reading just plain fun! And his influences stayed with his readers. When I was photographing high school and college graduation ceremonies, I can't tell you how many student speakers would end their speech with:

> "You have brains in your head. You have feet in your shoes. You can steer yourself any direction you choose. You're on your own. And you know what you know. And YOU are the one who'll decide where to go..."
>
> ### Dr. Seuss, Oh, the Places You'll Go!

So what if Theodor Seuss Geisel had been walking on the other side of the street in 1937? Or what if his Dartmouth friend had been delayed by traffic just a block earlier?

Luck – it's a part of our lives, but we do have to do the work prior to luck bumping into us in order for us to take advantage of it.

My son's girlfriend, Meredith, gave Ben a handmade painting that said "Make Your Own Luck."   Apparently it's a philosophy Ben had picked up from his job shadowing experience with Rob Dyrdek and is a philosophy that - now that I am aware of it-- many people share.

Making your own luck requires a commitment of time, energy and focus. It will require your son or daughter to recognize their priorities, understand the influences of society and draw a line in the sand on the balance they want to create in their lives. If they choose to include a strategic commitment to their career, they too will be able to take advantage of chance encounters with others that will launch them in directions they dreamed about, but never thought they could reach.

CAREER MANAGEMENT + HABIT+ LUCK = SUCCESS

It's a simple formula, but I can assure you it works!

Despite some of the gloomy statistics we've shared with you throughout this book, by adopting the ideas and concepts we discussed in this book, your graduate has an incredible future ahead of him or her.

Graduates are stepping into a world with enormous problems, but one with enormous resources. They are stepping into a world where the internet is bringing millions of minds together in mere instants to solve issues, problems and situations.   It's a miraculous time for them to leave their marks.

They have the potential to make important contributions to their families, communities, companies, religions and governments.

I thought it might be fun to end this book by looking at a few people who either attended college or graduated who, with a combination of hard work, persistence and luck, have reached the peak of their industries:

- Jeff Bezos, the founder of Amazon.com, which has revolutionized the way we shop, attended Princeton University, planning to study physics, but soon returned to his love of computers and graduated with a Bachelor's of Science in Electrical Engineering and Computer Science.

- Eva Longoria was a student at Texas A&M University-Kingsville where she completed a degree in kinesiology in 1998 before she became a desperate housewife.

- Will Ferrell actually studied at the University of Southern California where he completed a sports casting degree in 1989. His future role in the movie *Anchor Man* sounds like it was right up his alley!

- Gene Simmons majored in education at Richmond College on Staten Island and briefly taught elementary school before his band KISS led to decades of concert performances and a reality TV show. I doubt that we'll see him back teaching in an elementary school.

- Oprah Winfrey majored in speech and drama at Tennessee State University and upon graduation got a job as the first black anchor person on a local TV channel in Nashville. She's gone on touch the lives of millions of people every day.

- Ray Romano went to Queens College in Flushing, New York, where he studied accounting before he became the symbol of the changing American husband stereotype.

- Hugh Hefner who founded Playboy magazine majored in psychology at the University of Illinois, at Urbana-Champaign. His minor in writing and art came in handy in the magazine industry.

- Jodie Foster graduated *magna cum laude* with a bachelor's degree in literature from Yale University. She is a two-time Academy Award-winning American actress, director, and producer. She has also won two Golden Globes, BAFTA and a Screen Actors' Guild Award.

- Steve Martin majored in philosophy at Long Beach College (now California State University--Long Beach) and at UCLA.

He even briefly considered becoming a philosophy professor before turning to comedy.

- Mick Jagger was a business student at the rigorous London School of Economics when he, Keith Richards, and Brian Jones formed The Rolling Stones. He was still enrolled, even after the band started performing professionally.

I doubt if you asked any one of these entrepreneurs, actors and sports figures what they would be doing 10 years out of college, they would have had any idea. Most had passions, interest and an inner drive that – along with a bit of luck and a lot of hard work-- made them captains of their industries and household names.

Like the creator of Dr. Seuss, each of these public figures could tell you a similar story of the big break, the one event that literally changed his or her life. They, too, were walking down the right sides of the proverbial streets and they not only recognized the opportunities but were prepared to act on those when they were presented.

Your son or daughter has a good chance of being included in a list like this in the not too distant future. The opportunities to make a difference, build new businesses, support structures, and make the world a better place could not be better.

To get started, your child will need your help, encouragement and coaching to take ownership of his or her career and along the way build a plan and job search strategy.

Perhaps a final quote from Dr.Seuss sums it up best!

> *"The more that you read, the more things you will know. The more that you learn, the more places you'll go."*

Dr. Seuss, I can Read With My Eyes Shut!

SUMMARY

You've been there for your child for his or her entire life.

Now is not the time to sit back and assume the college will help your child choose the right career, build a career plan and learn proven job search strategies.

Your student will need your help in creating the habits necessary to build a successful career plan. Nothing you've done in the past will match the importance of this responsibility because these skills will stay with your child for the rest of his or her professional life. You know by now, the Department of Labor predicts they will have 11-14 jobs by the time they are 38 years old. It only makes sense to learn how to successfully look for a job now, so they can effortlessly slip out of one job and advance into the next one. If we do our job right, we'll be helping them to "Work smarter, not harder!"

COMING UP NEXT

You've picked up a lot of knowledge that will be of benefit to your student. In order to act on the opportunities you have to help your student, we've outlined some next steps for you.

All our dreams can come true...if we have the courage to pursue them.

- **Walt Disney**, Chief Imaginer!

YOUR TO DO'S AND NOTES!

CHAPTER RESOURCES

| *Visit Your College Career Center!* | **Parent Online Community**
www.theunemployedgrad.com | You and your grad are not the only ones going through this experience. Pick up ideas, tips and job leads from other parents who have students in college and recently graduated. |

12

NEXT STEPS

So there you have it!

The Unemployed Grad, And What Parents Can Do About It.

I'd like to congratulate you for finishing the book. Research suggests that 80 percent of books that were bought were never read. That must mean you feel passionate and are committed to doing whatever you can to help your son or daughter in his or her first professional job search.

By now you've realized what your responsibilities are and how you can be a resource to help your student/grad in his or her first professional career search.

It doesn't matter if he or she is just heading off to college, in college or recently graduated--the tips, ideas and strategies you now have will give you the knowledge to be a reliable resource for your child.

Here's what I'd like you to do next:

1. If you haven't done it already, download a copy of the companion workbook for this book and use it to help build a career management strategy with your student/grad. (Check the following resources page for details.)

2. If your son or daughter is in college, get to know what services are available in the career center and make sure your child takes advantage of them. At the same time, touch base with college administrators requesting they make career management a required activity prior to graduation.

3. Stop by www.yourcollegecareercenter.com and check out the courses, coaching and community of like-minded people who are working through the same strategies and ideas you are. <u>You don't have to travel this road alone!</u>

Finally, I encourage you to continue to educate yourself about the changes that are happening in the job search industry so that you can be ready to use your network and the sundry new tools to help you quickly move up the ladder to the next exciting position for yourself.

All the best to you and your student/grad,

Together, you both will be able to make the lives of all of those around you more rewarding, satisfying and productive.

Twenty years from now you will be more disappointed by the things you didn't do than by the ones you did. So throw off the bowlines, sail away from the safe harbor. Catch the trade winds in your sails. Explore. Dream. Discover.

- **Mark Twain**, Author

YOUR TO DO'S AND NOTES!

_____

_____

_____

_____

_____

_____

_____

_____

_____

_____

CHAPTER RESOURCES

| *Visit Your College Career Center!* | **The Unemployed Grad Workbook**

 www.theunemployedgrad.com | Essential Workbook provides exercises for each chapter that will help your student build a successful career plan and job search strategy. Free! |

Take advantage of the resources we've assembled to help you be a powerful asset to your student in developing a successful career plan and job search strategy for their first professional career search.

**You can get access to all resources at
www.theunemployedgrad.com**

The Unemployed Grad Workbook

Essential Workbook provides exercises for each chapter that will help your student build a successful career plan and job search strategy. Free!

Career Readiness Quiz

Most grads think they know what they need to do to search for a job. Here's a 100 question quiz that will help them see what they need to be working on today! Free!

Career Coach Webinars

You can gain the insights and advice of some of the top student/grad career coaches in the nation in these regularly scheduled webinars.

Parent Online Boot Camp & Parent Career Orientation Webinars

If your student is graduating, or a recent grad, you should participate in the Parent Online Boot Camp! For parents whose students are entering, or in college check out the Parent Career Orientation Webinars!

Grad Career Toolkit

You can give your graduate access to the essential Grad Career Toolkit that will include over 40 ideas, tips and tools that will help them get a job! Free!

Linkedin Primer for Grads

We'll show you how your grad should be using Linkedin to network with alumni and build relationships starting their freshman year! Free!

Career courses to prepare for job searches

Your student needs to master the fundamental job search skills. Check out the courses offered in building resumes, networking, interviewing, job search and more!

Free video on Guerilla Marketing techniques

We've assembled 20 unique, fun, yet proven techniques that will help your grad get the CAREER job they want! Free!

Hiring Manager Webinars

You and your student/grad can gain the insights and advice of some of the top hiring managers in the nation in these regularly scheduled webinars. Learn what they see, from their side of the desk!

News & Information

Register for our eNewsletter and blog to get a steady diet of inspiring ideas, confidence building advice and strategies to get jobs! Free!

Parent Online Community

You and your grad are not the only ones going through this experience. Pick up ideas, tips and job leads from other parents who have students in college and recently graduated.

ABOUT THE AUTHOR

Don Philabaum is one of the early pioneers in the online community industry. He founded a firm to develop online communities for students and alumni in 1996 and went on to build 300 online alumni communities around the globe. He's been driven by the desire to help institutions use their online communities to connect and engage members to help them do business, mentor, and get jobs. Don is co-founder of TalentMarks, a firm that provides cloud-based career curriculum for schools, students, grads and alumni that is delivered 24/7 through any device.

Contact info

donp@talentmarks.com

ww.talentmarks.com

800-849-1762 x 203

BOOKS, WHITEPAPERS AND WORKBOOKS BY DON PHILABAUM

Books

The Unemployed Grad, And What Parents Can Do About It!

Engage Customers Online

Internet Dough

Alumni Online Engagement

The Little Blue Book of Facebook

Create a Comprehensive College Internet Strategy

White Papers

10 Ways to Get More Resources for Your Career Center

Create a Career Centered College Culture and Curriculum

Admissions Social Media Assessment Guide

Facebook 101 for the Executive Suite

51 Facebook Content Strategies for Your Organization

Creating a Campus Fan Page Strategy

Tapping into the Social GRID with Facebook Apps

Six P's of Building Online Community

Add L.U.C.K to Your Online Community

Online Community in the Pioneer Days

Workbooks

Build a Social Media Strategy for Your College

Triple Registrations in Your Online Community

Create a Comprehensive Internet Strategy for Your Organization

VISIT YOUR COLLEGE
CAREER CENTER

FOR RESOURCES MENTIONED IN
THIS BOOK VISIT

WWW.THEUNEMPLOYEDGRAD.COM

GET THIS
COMPLIMENTARY WORKBOOK

DOWNLOAD AT
WWW.THEUNEMPLOYEDGRAD.COM

ACKNOWLEDGEMENT

My hope is your student and grad will have many business advisors, mentors and coaches in their life. I've been fortunate to have a number of people who have led by example, inspired me and or took the time to care about my dreams, goals and ambitions. Without their commitment of time and emotional involvement, I'm certain my life would have been vastly different.

Tom Costigan
Jack Counts
Dave Daywalt
Reverend Andrew Newberry
Jim Nichols
Nick Moulakis
Al Philabaum
Willis Wolfe

Thanks to you all!